OLD TESTAMENT GUIDES

General Editor

R.N. Whybray

THE SONG OF SONGS

THE SONG
OF SONGS

A. Brenner

Published by JSOT Press
for the Society for Old Testament Study

Published by JSOT Press
JSOT Press is an imprint of
Sheffield Academic Press Ltd
The University of Sheffield
343 Fulwood Road
Sheffield S10 3BP
England

Typeset by Sheffield Academic Press
and
printed in Great Britain
by Billing & Sons Ltd
Worcester

British Library Cataloguing in Publication Data available

ISSN 0264-6498
ISBN 1-85075-242-7

CONTENTS

88502

A PERSONAL NOTE

'The winter has gone, the rain is past. Blossoms appear in the land. . . The voice of the turtledove. . . the figs. . . the vines. . . ' We sang this song and similar ones every spring, from Kindergarten on. Later, when we became adolescents, there were songs about a 'shepherd' and a 'shepherdess', 'I am my lover's and he is mine', 'You are fair, my love, you are fair, your eyes are doves', 'Many waters cannot extinguish love'. And there were dances, 'I went down to the walnut garden. . . '. It finally dawned on me one Passover night when I already was well into my teens that the biblical words my father intoned Lithuanian-style, after the ceremonial dinner, were more than familiar: that I could recite most of the verses of the SoS at will, because I had been singing them unwittingly for as long as I could remember. The words of the SoS were mine before I realized that they were biblical. And spring meant—it still does, even at this very moment—a flood of *Shir Hashirim* text and melodies.

Writing about a text which has been part of my life ever since I can remember was a special pleasure. I thank Professor R.N. Whybray, the editor of the Old Testament Guides series, and the (British) Society for Old Testament Study for giving me the opportunity to do so.

This book is for Philip.

Haifa, Spring 1989   Athalya Brenner

ABBREVIATIONS

AB	Anchor Bible
ANET	J.B. Pritchard (ed.), *Ancient Near Eastern Texts*, 2nd edition, Princeton: Princeton University Press: 1955
BDB	F. Brown, S.R. Driver, C.A. Briggs, *Hebrew and English Lexicon of the Old Testament*, Oxford: Clarendon, 1972
BKAT	Biblischer Kommentar Altes Testament
CBQ	*Catholic Biblical Quarterly*
EJ	*Encyclopaedia Judaica*, Jerusalem, 1971
ETL	*Ephemerides Theologicae Lovanienses*
GK	E. Kautzsch (ed., trans. A.E. Cowley), *Gesenius' Hebrew Grammar*, Oxford: Clarendon, 1910 (reprinted 1966)
HAR	*Hebrew Annual Review*
IB	*Interpreter's Bible*
ICC	International Critical Commentary
IDB	*Interpreter's Dictionary of the Bible*
JAAR	*Journal of the American Academy of Religion*
JBL	*Journal of Biblical Literature*
JSOT	*Journal for the Study of the Old Testament*
JSS	*Journal of Semitic Studies*
OTL	Old Testament Library
VT	*Vetus Testamentum*
ZAW	*Zeitschrift für die alttestamentliche Wissenschaft*

General Reading

An asterisk (*) indicates works suitable for beginners.

The most comprehensive commentary available in English is:

M.H. Pope, *Song of Songs. A New Translation with Introduction and Commentary* (AB), Garden City, New York: Doubleday, 1977. The volume includes a comprehensive Introduction; three bibliographies (one on the text and its translations, one on pre-1800 critical literature, and one on post-1800 literature); a translation of the Hebrew text; critical notes; and indexes. The Introduction (pp. 17-229) is especially recommended for its survey of the main issues of the interpretation of the SoS, and for the history of interpretation through the ages.

Other helpful titles are:

*R. Gordis, *The Song of Songs and Lamentations*, New York: Ktav, 1977 (Revised edition). With a modern translation and commentary. Valuable for its commonsense approach and brevity.

*T.J. Meek, 'The Song of Songs' (*IB*, vol. V), New York and Nashville: Abingdon, 1956. With the King James Version (1611) and the Revised Standard Version (1946-1952) on the top part of each page. The Introduction (pp. 91-98) and the Exegesis (the middle part of each page) present a concise scholarly treatment. The Exposition (pp. 98-102 and, from there onwards, on the bottom third of each page) is homiletic, thus outside the scope of this OT Guide.

C.D. Ginsburg, *The Song of Songs and Coheleth*, ed. S.H. Blank, New York: Ktav, 1970 (=1857, 1861). Although many of the views advanced—especially those dealing with the framework for interpretation—are by now outdated, the commentary is worth using for its many insights and detailed philological comments.

*W.J. Fürst, *The Books of Ruth, Esther, Ecclesiates, The Song of Songs, Lamentations* (Cambridge Bible Commentaries), Cambridge: Cambridge University Press, 1975.

H.H. Rowley, 'The Interpretation of the Song of Songs'; in: *The Servant of the Lord and Other Essays*, Oxford: Blackwell, 1965, pp. 195-246. A valuable introduction to the main issues of interpretation.

In other languages, the following works are of importance:

In Hebrew:

Y. Feliks, *The Song of Songs: Nature, Epic, and Allegory*, Jerusalem: Keter, 1980.

In French:

A. Robert and J.R. Tournay, *Le Cantique des Cantiques: Traduction et Commentaire*, Paris: Gabalda, 1963.

D. Lys, *Le Plus Beau Chant de la Création*, Paris: Cerf, 1968.

In German:

G. Gerleman, *Ruth, Das Hohelied* (BKAT 18), Neukirchen-Vluyn: Neukirchener Verlag, 1965.

E. Würthwein, *Die Fünf Megilloth*, Tübingen: Mohr, 1969.

On Biblical Poetry:

E.R. Follis (ed.), *Directions in Biblical Hebrew Poetry*, Sheffield: JSOT, 1987.

J.L. Kugel, *The Idea of Biblical Poetry: Parallelism and its History*, New Haven, 1981.

W.G.E. Watson, *Classical Hebrew Poetry: A Guide to Its Techniques*, Sheffield: JSOT Press, 1984.

On poetic metaphors in general:

G. Lakoff and M. Turner, *More Than Cool Reason: A Field Guide to Poetic Metaphor*, Chicago and London: Chicago U.P., 1989.

And in the SoS:

H.P. Müller, *Vergleich und Metaphor im Hohelied*, Göttingen, 1984.

A Note on English Translations to the Song of Songs

It is almost impossible to capture the original flavour of the SoS in a different language because, in addition to the formidable difficulties of rendering poetry in general, it presents the translator with some particular problems: its language abounds with semantic and grammatical peculiarities; the division into individual poems is often debatable; the identification of voices (female, male, singular, plural) and form (monologue, dialogue, concerted response) is not always easy; the metphors are rich and multifaceted; there are many changes of levels of diction, mood and tone; and the poetic metres employed defy reproduction in another language. Finally, the subject of love invites a pronounced personal attitude, conscious or otherwise, on the part of the translator(s).

Therefore, if one reads the SoS in English translation, it is preferable to use at least two translations jointly for any given passage. Initially, the division into male-female voices, customarily added in some of the translations, should be ignored until verified by reading the text.

Here is a partial list of some of the translations available. The King James Version and the RSV are, of course, classical. Some modern translations worth consulting are:

The New English Bible, Oxford—Cambridge, 1970.

The Jerusalem Bible (A. Jones, ed.), London: Darton, Longman & Todd; Garden City, New York: Doubleday, 1966.

H.L. Ginsberg, *The Five Megilloth and Jonah: A New Translation*, Philadelphia: Jewish Publication Society of America, 1969.

Pope and Gordis include translations in their commentaries (see above). To these the following should be added:

M. Falk, *Love Lyrics from the Bible: A Translation and Literary Study of the Song of Songs*, Sheffield: Almond, 1982. A highly personal and poetic attempt to recapture the sense of the Hebrew original rather than its literary meanings, and to reproduce it in English poetry. The Hebrew text is reprinted alongside the translation. Pages 54-133 deal with the problems of translation and with literary aspects of the SoS.

M.V. Fox, *The Song of Songs and the Ancient Egyptian Love Songs*, Madison: University of Wisconsin, 1985. An attractive and readable translation; annotated.

M.D. Goulder, *The Song of Fourteen Songs*, JSOT: Sheffield, 1986. The text is readable and substantiated by notes. The structural division into fourteen poems and its implications, however, should be approached with caution.

Note: After a bibliographical entry has been cited in full for the first time, subsequent references to it will be in an abbreviated form—either by author's name alone, or by author and brief title.

OVERVIEW

1. The Title and the Place
of the Book in the Hebrew Canon

The first verse of the SoS is a superscription that functions both as a title to the book and an editorial comment on it. It has three components: the actual name of the book, Hebrew *šyr hšš̆yrym*, literally 'Poem of the Poems'; the relative pronoun *'šr*, followed by the preposition *lᵉ*; and the proper name 'Solomon', which refers to the King of that name. All three components are problematic, for each can sustain more than one interpretation.

An understanding of the grammatical structure of the title would supply an insight into the literary nature of the book (at least according to the editor's views, as they are exemplified in the work). The superscription not only reflects the editor's or editors' views of the material but has also, in itself, conditioned the views of generations of readers. Its intrinsic ambivalence must therefore be investigated, and its implications examined.

The SoS is one of the Five Scrolls, a collection which forms part of the Writings (Kethubim), the third division of the Hebrew Bible. Since this was the last part of the Bible to become canonized, the placement of the SoS within it indicates the relative lateness of the book. It thus supports the assignment of its date to some time after the first Exile, during the era of the Second Commonwealth.

The book's subject matter is erotic (young) love of the non-marital kind. It is secular, does not express national sentiments, and contains no ideologically motivated allusions to religious or ethical values. Hence, the Jewish sages were divided over the reasons and justifications for its acceptance into the Hebrew Canon. There can hardly be any doubt that the attribution of its composition to king Solomon played a part in the process of acceptance. Another factor was probably the popularity of the poems and their wide distribution. The chief reason for the book's canonization, however, must have been the endorsement of its religious, allegorical interpretation as the officially valid exegesis. By the second century CE the allegorical interpretation had gained ground to such an extent that the book was accepted into the orthodox teachings of both Judaism and Christianity, so much so that its literal meaning was hardly discussed as such until the nineteenth century: the originally secular love lyrics became an exemplification of and a hyperbole for God's affinity with His people (in orthodox as well as mystical Judaism) and Christ's relationship with the Church.

2. The Text: Matter and Form

The SoS, as we shall presently see, is best viewed as a collection of love lyrics rather than as a single poem (although a number of scholarly voices, in the past and in the present, advocate its unity). The poems are strung together by associative links and, first and foremost, by the subject and subject matter.

Love, and its literal expressions, has many faces. Some of its features are more pronounced in the SoS than others. The love is unmarried love, and—some interpretations of the book notwith-standing (see below, Chapter 8)—marriage is not necessarily envisaged as its ultimate objective, although sexual consummation is. It is outspokenly erotic and sexual. The love relationships depicted are confident and free of jealousy (with the possible exception of 8.6). A variety of loving moods is evident, from the serious and passionate to the teasing and humorous.

Most of the poems are delivered through the poetic convention of an 'I', a first person voice that can be either female or male. The poems thus form monologues or dialogues, sometimes completed with remarks by, or conversations with, a female or male chorus.

One of the reasons for viewing the SoS as a collection of poems is the absence of a unified, typical, or single style. It is thus best to describe the poetic devices which define the poems individually within the traditions of biblical poetry, instead of trying to find detailed common denominators for the whole work. The conventional formal devices used are similar to those that feature in other instances of biblical and other poetry. They include parallelism; refrains; repetitions of roots, words, and expressions; puns, word play and sound play; rhythm; and rhyme.

The heavy use of metaphorical and symbolical language is typically poetic too. The language of the SoS actually achieves the impossible: it is conventional but, at the same time, original. The metaphors and symbols are drawn from many fields of human activity and custom—urban and rural life, zoology, botany, geography, and others. Some are recurrent symbols and metaphors. Among those one may list the garden/vineyard/orchard metaphor, the gazelle, the dove, certain flowers, aromatics and perfumes, walls and fortifications. In each case, the thematic values of the metaphors are crucial for the understanding of the poem(s) in which they feature.

Love poems may be quite vague in regard to their original setting and background, a feature which contributes to their universal appeal. The SoS is no exception. Although it contains many allusions to geographical, social and natural factors, it lacks specificity as to its original setting(s). When and where was it composed? When and where was it compiled and/or edited? When did the poems become a collection, and for what purpose? Also, the collection was presumably sung or recited on certain recurrent social occasions. We shall try to examine what those occasions might have been before and after the endorsement of the religious-allegorical interpretation, which transported the SoS and its recitation from the secular to the sacral plane.

3. Unity and Sequence, or an Anthology? Individual Poems and Literary Structure

Whether we accept the opinion that the SoS is a collection of poems (as is done here), or see it as a unified composition, two basic questions have to be dealt with. The first is: How can the boundaries of the individual poetic units be recognized? This question is not easy to answer, since the poems were apparently arranged by associative chains relating to contents and/or form and, in numerous cases, simply 'run' into each other to the point of fusion; whereas, in other cases, no principle of association is recognizable. This leads us to the second question: Even after an attempt is made to delineate the individual poems, can the principle of organization that informs the whole collection be uncovered? In other words, is the SoS an *anthology* of love lyrics or, alternatively, a *sequence*?

The first alternative implies a loose linkage of the individual poems through thematic or verbal associations, or both, in a more or less random external manner. Accordingly, the collection hinges on its theme and subject matter—erotic love—but is not designed along a linear plot. The second alternative postulates a general plot, with the repetitions of certain poems and expressions viewed as meaningful repetitions that advance the plot.

Each of these views has scholarly opinion to support it. Various principles of association can certainly account, at least in part, for the delineation of individual poems and for their linkage. On the other hand, we shall see that assigning an overall plot to the SoS seems more than a trifle forced. Nonetheless, some extended units (which are made up of smaller individual poems) seem to exhibit a mini-plot, an organised structure that relates to a cluster of events. A surface structural unity, one that is finally reconcilable with conceptual and verbal processes of association, albeit not with the notion of a comprehensive plot ('beginning, middle, end'!), appears to be the less problematic choice. In other words, the SoS is not a love story; it is a collection of love lyrics whose theme lends it integrity, but not narrative unification.

4. Extrabiblical Parallels

Heterosexual erotic love is widely acknowledged as a psycho-social factor in most cultures. Love poetry is one of the manifestations of this cultural acknowledgement (if not always approval). Finding thematic parallels for the SoS is, therefore, far from difficult. The problem is how to organize the parallels so that they contribute to our understanding of the SoS as a unique artistic achievement on the one hand, and as a product and reflection of its cultural environment on the other hand.

Parallels and themes corresponding to the love lyrics of the SoS are usually organized by scholars along two axes, the chronological (ancient to modern) and the spatial (locality: where the parallel originates from). The secular and liturgical love lyrics of Egypt, Mesopotamia, Ugarit, India, and Arabia have been cited for ancient times and places. Palestinian, Syrian, and Arabic love poetry from the 19th century up to the present are also cited. A brief survey shows that not many of the so-called parallels—be they either specific (correspondences in imagery and metaphorical language) or more general (similarity of motifs, the utilization of identical or similar genres, similar types of poetic sequence)—go beyond the level of thematic parity. In other words, the emotions and their literary expressions might be similar, as dictated by the universality of love.

But even in the case of ancient traditions of love poetry, a direct or mutual influence between the latter and the SoS is mostly difficult to establish. What remains, then, is to point out the correspondences and resemblances in the formal conventions, and the similar emotions reflected in the SoS and in other cultures and languages.

5. Daily Life and the Environment

Because of its subject, diversity and relatively open attitudes, the SoS is a source of abundant information about the social and natural contexts underlying it. The information is incidental to the main concerns of the poems, hence all the more valuable for not being tendentious.

Among the natural and cultural aspects of life which are referred to in passing are: forces of nature and seasonal changes; geography; fauna and flora, wild and cultured; economics, from agriculture to commerce; human professions and skills; building and fortification; morality and social institutions; the family; art and aesthetics. The information, from the nomenclature to the actual descriptions (be they literal, symbolical, or metaphorical), is a rich source for knowledge about the world of the SoS, that is, the biblical world.

6. The Language and Dating of the Book

The language of the SoS is an admixture of early and late linguistic features. It shows influence of Aramaic but, otherwise, only few foreign words or structures. How, then, should it be classified and dated? And, consequently, how should the entire book be dated?

Poetic language, and especially its vocabulary, often appears to be archaic or archaistic when compared with prose of similar periods and backgrounds. This is certainly true in the case of the SoS, where numerous words and grammatical formations can be ascribed to early classical (pre-exilic) biblical Hebrew, words and formations that became obsolete during later biblical times. Nonetheless, many other linguistic phenomena—of semantics as well as phonology, morphology and syntax—must be understood against the backdrop of Mishnaic Hebrew and Imperial Aramaic, hence belong to late (post-exilic) Biblical Hebrew. Furthermore, the influence of the Northern Israelite dialect must also be considered, in view of the several passages which impart an intimate knowledge of Northern realia through a language that, when compared with other biblical passages, seems full of linguistic peculiarities.

Late linguistic phenomena, their frequency and distribution within a text, are more important for the dating of that text than early phenomena, since late texts may naturally contain earlier features (whereas the reverse is rarer). Thus, the late linguistic features of the SoS point to a relatively late date of its composition or, at the very least, of its compilation and editing.

Another consideration for determining the nature and date of the book is the distinction between the language of individual poems, whose boundaries are not always easy to define, and that of the composition as a whole. Again, a later composition might include earlier pieces, while the opposite is less probable.

After marshalling the linguistic evidence, we shall see that a late date for the compilation of the whole composition, together with earlier ones for some individual poems, is accepted by most scholars. This fits in with the information about daily life and realia imparted in the SoS. Finally, the dating has a direct bearing on the question of the authorship of the book.

7. Authorship: Who 'Wrote' the SoS?

According to the historically prevalent interpretation of the super-scription (1.1) and Jewish tradition, the SoS is attributed to King Solomon. This is impossible to accept for linguistic as well as other reasons. Who, then, is the author/compiler of the book?

It has been stated already that the SoS is a collection of love lyrics strung together by theme and through association. It is made up of poems of various styles, varied backgrounds, and different dates. The author/compiler must have been well-informed and well-educated to collect such an anthology. He/she probably undertook some editing of his/her material; this explains the loose overall framework and a certain cohesion which the book has (however we choose to define that cohesion: see Chapter 8, 'Comprehensive Interpretations'). The identity of the person responsible for the collection cannot be uncovered. His/her date, however, must be later than the Persian period.

There is a growing tendency nowadays to assign the SoS to a female author or authors. This would explain various recurrent features in the work, such as the prominence of the female figures (see Chapter 10, 'Feminist Readings').

8. Theories of Comprehensive Interpretation

The interpretations discussed under this heading share several assumptions which underline the procedure of exegesis. These are: (a) The SoS is not just a collection put together by an editor/compiler, but a unified composition with a central plot and a message; and (b) the whole composition, when correctly interpretated, is more than simply the sum of its parts. At the present time, many scholars tend to attribute to the book editorial unity only: such scholars uphold the notion that the SoS should be interpreted verbally—that is, without looking for a concealed 'deeper' meaning—and viewed as an anthology of love lyrics. Accordingly, no 'comprehensive' interpretation of it is possible. The comprehensive interpretations introduced below therefore either represent past endeavours of scholarship and devotional activity, or else modern attempts to recoup some general plan for the composition as a whole.

The interpretations surveyed will be grouped under three headings: allegorical-symbolical, dramatic, cultic. The 'verbal' (not necessarily comprehensive) interpretation is introduced in Chapter 3.

9. Intertextual Connections:
The SoS within the Biblical Context

The secularity and a-historical character of the book, together with the absence of national and religious biases, make it unique within the Hebrew Bible. Its subject matter, erotic love, is not accorded such a comprehensive treatment anywhere else within the Old Testament. Still, love and pair-bonding are mentioned elsewhere, direcly as well as metaphorically. Three lines of investigation were here chosen for demonstrating intertextual affinities between the SoS and other biblical passages.

Proceeding from the level of the subject matter, the SoS should be related to a certain genre of prophetic tradition—passages in Hosea, Jeremiah, Ezekiel and the Second Isaiah, in which the relationship between God and His people is depicted in terms of a love story gone astray between a husband and wife.

Secondly, the accomplished poetics of the book point to a long tradition of poetry-making in many forms, poetry that was probably sung to or accompanied by music. Poetry, and its performance, is normally associated with the Israelite Wisdom tradition and its extant literature in the Bible. The relevant passages to be compared with the SoS are from the Psalms, Proverbs, and Qoheleth.

Finally, the garden/bower imagery of the SoS invites a consideration of its affinities with the lost Garden of Eden image (Gen. 2.4b–3). This will be discussed in more detail in the next section, since much of the interesting work on it stems from feminist criticism of the bible.

10. Feminist Readings of the SoS

For the purpose of the present study, a 'feminist reading' will be: (a) a reading that is sympathetic to the role women play within the literary framework of the SoS; and (b) analyses which expose androcentric (male centred) biases in the book and in its exegesis; and attempts to redress the discriminatory social balance reflected in biblical literature through a different way of criticism.

The points chosen for discussion as examples of feminist readings are: gender imagery in the SoS; the nature of the dream sequences (chs. 3 and 5); recognition of the centrality of the female figure(s); the link between the SoS and the Garden of Eden narratives; and the assignment of female authorship to the book, or parts thereof.

11. The SoS in Jewish and Christian Liturgy

The SoS has been linked to the Passover festival since the eighth century CE at the latest, although the exact time of its recitation during the festival varies. In some Jewish communities it is also recited every Friday.

In Christian Liturgy, the Latin (Vulgate) text of the book is included in the Marian festivities, and is accompanied by music.

12. The SoS in Music and the Visual Arts

The SoS and, more frequently, parts of it have been set to music by various composers.

In the plastic arts, a distinction should be made between two categories: illuminations or illustrations of the text on the one hand; and artistic compositions inspired by the poems on the other hand.

Further Reading

The following works contain brief and illuminating introductions to most of
the issues presented in the Overview:

S.R. Driver, *An Introduction to the Literature of the Old Testament*,
9th edn. Edinburgh: T. & T. Clark, 1913 (reprinted
Cleveland and New York: Meridian, 1963), pp. 436-53.

*O. Eissfeldt, *The Old Testament: An Introduction* (trans. P.R.
Ackroyd), Oxford: Blackwell, 1966, pp. 483-91.

*G. Fohrer (trans. D. Green), *Introduction to the Old Testament*,
New York and Nashville. Abingdon, 1968, pp. 299-303.

*R.H. Pfeiffer, *Introduction to the Old Testament*, New York:
Harper, 1948; London: Black, 1957.

*N.K. Gottwald, 'Song of Songs', in *IDB*, New York and Nashville:
Abingdon, 1962, vol. IV, pp. 42-26.

*K.N. Schoville, 'Song of Songs', in *EJ*, Jerusalem: Keter, 1971,
vol. XV, pp. 144-50.

F. Landy, 'The Song of Songs', in R. Alter and F. Kermode (eds.),
The Literary Guide to the Bible, Cambridge, Mass.:
Harvard U.P., 1987, pp. 305-19.

A solid well-organized introduction in Hebrew, with a good classified
bibliography, is:

*S.M. Paul, 'Shir Hashirim (The Song of Songs)', in *Encyclopaedia
Biblica*, Jerusalem: Bialik, 1981, vol. VII, pp. 645-55.

Two other works in Hebrew are:

E. Levinger, *Shir Hashirim (The Song of Songs)*, Jerusalem,
1973.

M. Fox and J. Klein (eds.), 'Shir Hashirim (The Song of Songs)', in
The World of the Bible Encyclopaedia, Ramat Gan:
Revivim, 1988, vol. XVIa, pp. 11-68.

1

THE TITLE OF THE BOOK
AND ITS PLACE IN
THE HEBREW CANON

The Superscription (1.1)

THE SUPERSCRIPTION is usually rendered, almost literally, 'The Song of Songs of Solomon', 'The Song of Songs, which is Solomon's' (AV, RSV), 'Canticles' (from Latin), or something similar. The meaning of the title, however, requires clarification. Does it mean that the book should be viewed as a single 'song' (poem) or, on the contrary, several 'songs' (poems)? Or does the strange compound 'Song of Songs' have another meaning? Furthermore, the 'of' is a translation of the Hebrew relative pronoun '*šr*; and the preposition *lᵉ*, which appears in the titles of many Psalms too, may denote here as well as there the more frequent 'of, belonging to' but also 'by', 'for', 'concerning', or 'about' (Solomon). 'Solomon' is King Solomon, son of David; are we told, then, that the book was composed by Solomon, which will determine its authorship and set its date of composition in the tenth century BCE—or merely about Solomon as a figure in the poem(s), which leaves the question of the authorship and date of the book open for the time being?

The single appearance of the relative pronoun '*šr*, which is elsewhere in the book substituted by its later equivalent *š*-, defines the superscription as external to the work itself. Thus 1.1 constitutes an editorial comment, meant to guide us towards an understanding of the literary nature of the book, its author and its date of composition. Such a comment might be accepted as authoritative. One may, however, question it.

Jewish tradition of course accepted the authority of the super-scription and interpreted the preposition *lᵉ*- as 'of', and attributed the authorship of the SoS to King Solomon (together with the books of Proverbs and Qoheleth). However, the variety of meanings carried by the preposition *l^e*- makes it impossible to know whether that indeed was the editor's intention. We shall later see why these traditional views about Solomonic date and authorship for the book cannot be accepted for literary and linguistic reasons (Chapters 6 and 7 below).

The compound *šyr hššyrym*, 'Song of Songs', is a superlative. It literally means 'the best song', 'the most sublime song' (cf. Pope's translation for the phrase). Other biblical expressions for conveying a superlative through the same grammatical structure are, among others, 'holy of holies' (Exod. 26.33) and 'king of kings' (Ezek. 26.7). In these and other instances, a single entity is defined by a superlative structure. The title therefore implies that the editor/compiler who assigned it viewed the work as a single, unified poem—an issue which will be discussed in Chapters 3 and 7 below.

The Place of the Book in the Hebrew Bible

In the printed Hebrew editions, the SoS is the first of the Five Megilloth (Scrolls), a collection which is part of the third division of the Hebrew Bible, the *kethubim* ('Writings'). However, the Talmud (*Baba Bathra* 14b, 15a; *Berakhot* 57b), together with Hebrew manuscripts of the Bible and early printed editions of it, show that initially the SoS was placed elsewhere within the Writings, at times together with the two other biblical books whose authorship is attributed to King Solomon (Proverbs and Qoheleth). Manuscripts of the Greek Version (the Septuagint) also attest to two different arrangements. It seems that the book's current position as the first of the Megilloth is determined by its Jewish liturgical reading on Passover (see Chapter 11).

Canonicity and Canonization

The collection of The Writings was the last part of the Bible to become canonized; it was in fact still somewhat fluid at the beginning of the Christian Era. Therefore, the placing of the SoS among the Writings indicates that a relatively late date of composition should be assigned to it (Chapter 6).

There is no clear evidence for a canonical status of the SoS before the Christian Era. Neither Ben Sira (47.15) nor Josephus (*Against Apion* 1.8) refers to it directly when listing the books of Scripture.

The Mishna and Tosefta attest to the discussion, in Rabbinical circles during the second century CE, about its canonicity. It is difficult, however, to determine whether the objections to the book imply a dispute over its already accomplished inclusion in the Jewish Canon, or an actual process of canonization in progress. Eventually, mainly through the influence of the Hillel school and Rabbi Aqiba in particular, it was fully accepted and regarded as canonical and sacred (not to be sung at banquet houses, that is, used for profane enjoyment). In the Babylonian Talmud (*Baba Bathra* 14) it is simply enumerated among the sacred books. Around the time of the Jewish deliberations about the canonicity of the book, the Church accepted it as Scripture as well.

The traditional attribution of the composition of the SoS to King Solomon was undoubtedly one of the reasons for its acceptance as part of the Hebrew canon. Another reason, equally convincing probably, was its popularity: although the SoS is the only extensive sample of Hebrew love poetry from biblical times that has survived, there is every reason to assume that this literary genre was as popular then as the emotions it celebrates. The decisive factor, though, seems to have been the adoption of the allegorical interpretation of the SoS as official teaching within both Judaism and Christianity. The discussions in the Jewish sources (in the Mishna—Tractate *Yadayim* 3.5 and *The Fathers according to Rabbi Nathan* 1; in the Tosefta— *Yadayim* 2.4, *Sanhedrin* 12.10; in the Babylonian Talmud—*Sanhedrin* 101a, *Baba Bathra* 14-15) point to this understanding of the process. So does the evidence of the Aramaic Targum (translation) to the SoS (a *midrash* on the Hebrew text rather than a proper literal translation), the Haggadic elaboration of the SoS (Song of Songs Rabbah, see 1.11) and, consequently, the mainstream Jewish exegesis of medieval times (Rashi). By the second century CE, then, the process was accomplished. The SoS became Scripture, but at the cost of the suppression of its original meaning and setting in life— that of secular love poetry.

Further Reading

For the superscription and the place of the SoS in the Hebrew canon, see the commentaries by Pope and Gordis, and the introductory literature cited at the end of the Overview. On the grammatical notion of the 'superlative' conveyed by compounds like *šyr hššyrym*, 'song of songs', see GK, section 132i.

On the canonization and the canonical status of the SoS, the English translations available for the relevant Hebrew sources are:

For the Mishna:

> H. Danby, *The Mishna*, London: Milford, 1938;
> L. Finkelstein, *The Fathers according to Rabbi Nathan*, 1955; or
> J. Neusner, *Aboth de-Rabbi Nathan*, Atlanta: Scholars Press, 1986.

For the Tosefta:

> H. Danby, *Tractate Sanhedrin, Mishna and Tosefta*, London, 1919.

For the Babylonian Talmud:

> I. Epstein (ed.), *The Babylonian Talmud*, London: Soncino, vol. XI (*Baba Bathra*), pp. 70f. and vol. XII, pp. 684f. (*Sanhedrin*).

For the Song of Songs Rabbah:

> M. Simon in the series *The Soncino Midrash*, London, 1939.

2

THE TEXT: MATTER AND FORM

The SoS—Love Lyrics

THE SOS IS WIDELY defined by readers and critics as 'love poetry'. Each of the two components of the definition, 'love' (for the content) and 'poetry' (for the literary form and format), should be clarified before proceeding further.

Love is the subject matter of the SoS. But what love, what manifestations of love? What love relationships are referred to? To begin with, it is heterosexual. One salient feature is the secular nature of that love. The lovers, male and female, are at least equal within the relationship; in fact, the female/s is/are the predominant partner/s (Trible). Mutual sexuality is celebrated without shame. The love relationship and its consummation is viewed as an end in itself: marriage is not necessarily the ultimate objective of the courtships. It is sentimental and romantic, in the sense that at times the lover of either sex is being adored to the point of idealization. Basically, though, the love spoken about is sensual and erotic. If the description of erotic activity, aspired for or accomplished, in general falls short of vulgarity, it is because of the subtle use of metaphorical and symbolical language. For example, the thinly veiled allusions to the female lover as an orchard (1.6) or garden entered by the male lover (4.10-5.1); the employment of aromatics and perfumes as symbols for female (4.6; 5.5) and male (1.3, 12-13) sexuality; and the fruit symbolism (2.3; 7.8-9; 8.2b) are perhaps even more effective than the more explicit references to physical love (2.6=8.3; 1.16). Such veiled allusions have added advantages, of course—they are evocative and, at the same time, more acceptable socially than explicit references.

The moods depicted and, consequently, the tone vary greatly. They extend from the serious and passionate (3.1-4; 6.4; 8.6) to the teasing and humorous (1.8; 7.1-10; 8.9). The only emotion associated with love absent from the SoS is jealousy, mentioned in 8.6 but not practised. In sum, then, the love depicted is an active relationship—especially on the part of the female lover—, a basically fulfilling experience if not always easy to handle (see especially the female search scenes, 1.7-8; 3.1-4; 5.6-7; and the female lover's pinings for the male, 2.5; 8.1-2a).

Now to the second component, the definition of the SoS as 'poetry' or 'lyrics'. In the Hebrew (Masoretic) text of the SoS, 'Poetic units are not apparent: no demarcation is given for individual poems, stanzas, or lines of verse. In other words, the text looks like a mass of prose on the page, divided only into sections and subsections of approximately equal length. Theoretically, then, the Song might be *seen* as having no poetic structure at all. . . . Yet no one disagrees that the Song is poetry, not prose. This is because of its *audibly* apparent rhythms. . . and its style' (Falk, p. 67). As Falk says, the SoS is considered 'poetic' because of its style, because its themes are expressed through a series of poetic devices (recognizable when compared with other poetic biblical passages). These devices will be listed below. And yet, since the book lacks the formal layout we are used to in poetry, such as the spatial arrangement of lines and stanzas on the page, it is often difficult to determine where a certain poetic unit ends and another begins. This difficulty is a serious handicap for the interpretation as well as the translation of the SoS (Chapter 3 below).

The Cast: Figures and Characterization

The lyrics of the SoS are delivered through the convention of speaking voices; that is, as in a play or a series of playlets. Some of the poems are constructed as monologues (scenes in which only one person addresses an audience through the point of view of an 'I'—for example, 1.2b-4, addressed to a second person); or as soliloquies (speaking one's thoughts aloud, even when no addressee is present—for example, 1.16, which refers to the lover in the third person). Others are constructed as dialogues (1.7-8).

The speakers/players are:

a.   Female speakers who assume the persona of a lover.
b.   Male speakers who assume the persona of a lover.

Because the SoS is viewed here as a collection of love poetry rather than a single unified composition, it is not possible to define the female and male voices as belonging to one female and one male persona only. Rather, a plurality of voices should be looked for: several loving couples, linked by the common theme.

c. A female chorus, the Daughters of Jerusalem, who function as an audience of listeners and/or speakers (2.7; 3.5; 5.8-9, 16; 6.1).

d. Two male choruses, one possibly within the scene of the dance (7.1-10), and the other a chorus of a woman's brothers (8.8-9).

In general, the literary figures of the female lovers (a) are characterized by their words as more forward, imaginative, articulate, and serious about the love relationship than their male counterparts. The males (b) are articulate enough, but also light-hearted and teasing (cf. the dialogue in 1.7-8, and ch. 7). Interestingly, the same division of emotional energy applies to Egyptian love poetry too (Fox, and Chapter 4 below). Also, in terms of stage exposure, so to speak, the female personas get preferential treatment, for more lines are spoken by females than by males (Brenner). Similarly, the space occupied by the female chorus is larger than that allotted to male choruses. The predominance of the female figures will be taken up again in Chapter 10.

What can we glean from the monologues and dialogues about the lovers and their relationship? To begin with, it seems from various clues (geographical, social, environmental) that more than one couple is implied: there is too much diversity in the portrayal of the lovers to assume that only one loving pair is depicted. Most commentators point out that the lovers are of a relatively tender age (Fox), since marriage and material considerations do not seem to occupy their thoughts while passion, physical appearances and external attributes do. There is an intrinsic confidence in the relationship(s), even though external (societal, 5.7) and internal (psychological) difficulties are acknowledged. The dark side of love is present too. Its final definition invokes death, the water of chaos, fire and perhaps God (8.6): as Landy points out, this, when all is said and done, is the credo of the SoS (Landy, p. 133).

The lover's designations for each other are *dwd*—'lover', 'loved one', 'brother' (for the male); 'dove', 'perfect one', 'sister', 'bride' (for the female—although, in respect to the last of these epithets, no marital status seems to be intended). The searching for and the seeking of the beloved is a recurrent theme. The choruses, somewhat like the chorus in a Greek play, serve as witnesses to the drama which is not theirs, a drama whose main characters are the lovers themselves.

Poetic Forms

As noted above, the lyrics of the SoS appear in the forms of monologue, soliloquy, and dialogue. Falk (p. 73) classifies the poems in more detail into three types of monologue, two types of dialogue, and one 'composite' poem.

One poetic genre which stands out is the *waṣf* (an Arabic term meaning 'description'). This type of poem refers to the lover's body, male or female, through a series of images and, usually, follows a certain pattern. Thus in 4.1-7 a female lover is invoked from the head downwards; and in 5.10-16 a male figure is described in the same order. A fragment of a *waṣf* that is almost identical to 4.1-3 is to be found in 6.3-7 (for the head and face only). A *waṣf* of the female body—this time proceeding in the opposite direction, from toe to head—is 7.1-7. All three complete *waṣfs* are ring constructions: they open (4.1=6.4a, 5.10; 7.2) and close (4.7; 5.16; 7.7) with a general remark about the pleasantness and desirability of the object of love.

The imagery of the *waṣf* is extravagant and sensuous. Its appropriateness, however, is not always evident, nor is its thematic intention. Presumably, a lover's physique is being described; yet, despite the richness of the imagery or because of it, it is impossible to visualize the figures described so imaginatively. What is finally conveyed to the reader is the poetic speaker's mood and desire rather than the aesthetic appearance of the object of love. Consequently, the *waṣf* poems, their imagery and emotive content, have been much debated by biblical scholars and often, as Falk points out, misunderstood. Pope cites many examples of *waṣf*-type poems from Arabic and other sources. Additional critical literature for this poetic genre is listed at the end of this chapter.

The Style: Poetic Features

The stylistic devices which feature in the SoS and define it as poetry do not differ substantially from those found in other poetic passages of the Hebrew Bible. Correspondences for each can be found elsewhere. Together, nonetheless, they constitute a stylistic—technical profile that makes the lyrics of the SoS unique. A few of these devices are listed here, with examples cited from the text.

(a) *Parallelism, metre and rhythm.* The basic unit is a parallel couplet (two 'stichs' which form a symmetrical unit, a 'line'). Less frequently, a line comprises more than a couplet (e.g. 1.3, 8). The couplets and lines are short, and words or closely-bound expressions are counted as metrical units. See Geller: 1979 for metre and parallelism in biblical poetry.

(b) *Rhyming* is occasional only and usually internal, within a stich (5.7) or between stichs of the same unit (4.5, 9).

(c) *Refrains and recurrent expressions* are characteristic of biblical poetry. Thus the dream poem of 3.1-4 is constructed round the repetition of two elements—'(the one) whom I love' appears in every verse; and the refrain 'I searched for him, but did not find him' appears twice, then changes to 'I found him' at the end of the poem (v. 4). The female lover is addressed by the words 'You are fair, my love, you are fair. Your eyes are doves' twice (1.15=4.1a). That the male lover's 'left hand is under my head and his right hand embraces me', is asserted twice by a woman (2.6=8.3). Three times the Daughters of Jerusalem are adjured by the gazelles and hinds not to awaken love until it is ready (the full text in 2.7=3.5; a shorter version also in 8.4). Other correspondences, or repeated couples of verses, are 2.9=8.14; 2.16=6.3; 4.3b=6.7; 4.2=6.6. The occurrence of most of the repeated verses either in the first or second halves of the book respectively points to the possibility of an intentional chiastic (inverted) structure for the whole. Some scholars (Exum, Landy) interpret the repetitions thus placed as clues to the unity of the whole composition. Others believe that the overall structure may equally be the result of the skilful compilation (Falk; see next chapter).

(d) Use of *similes and metaphors* from many areas of human experience (see Chapter 6). Several of these are developed into extended metaphors (hyperboles), and function as recurrent symbols. Such symbols are, for instance: the garden/orchard/vineyard imagery; the association of the male lover with particular flowers (lotus? 2.16

= 6.3) and animals (young deer, 2.17 and elsewhere), the female with others (lily? crocus?—2.1-2; dove—2.14; 5.2); the erotics denoted by perfumes for both male (1.3) and female (3.6; 4.13-14); the fortification/wall imagery for the female (6.10; 8.9-10). As in the case of the verbal repetitions mentioned in (c), the recurrence of certain symbols has a bearing on the problem of the structure.

(e) Another type of repetition is the *repetition of a particular sound*, or of groups of sounds, within a small poetic unit. Such repetitions are characteristic of the 'extended' unit, that is, one that has more than two lines. Thus a root is repeated in 1.2 ('kiss' [verb]. . . 'kisses' [noun]), in 2.14 (the root *r'h*, 'see' three times, in various formations), and elsewhere. Whole words are repeated twice or more within a couplet or verse—'foxes' in 2.15; *lbbtny*, 'you touched my heart' in 4.9; and further instances in 4.10 ('your love'), 7.1 ('come back'), 8.6 ('seal'), and elsewhere. A sequence of words is repeated in 1.15 ('you are fair'), 2.10 and 13 ('arise . . . and go'), and 3.1-4 (see p. 31 above).

(f) *Sound-play and word-play* (puns). Repetition of identical sounds within a small literary unit—whether consonants, vowels or groups of sounds—and play upon the different semantic meanings of similar or identical sound sequences are as frequent in the SoS as in many other biblical passages. It seems that, by and large, sound- and word-play are motivated by a sense of linguistic fun: they are affectations, a kind of intellectual game. Beyond this general notion, the reader is urged to consult the commentaries for the specific values of each type and occurrence of phonetic and semantic play.

Examples of alliteration (repetition of a consonant: the /š/ sound in 1.1-2a; 4.5) and assonance (repetition of vowel sounds—the /u/ sound in 5.7) are quite numerous. Another type of sound-play can be seen in the proximity of the verbs *nšq*, 'kiss' and *šqh*, 'cause to drink' (8.1-2), which differ by one consonant only. A possible double entendre is achieved in the use of the oblique *nhrw*, in the general sense of 'were angry' (1.6); and *šlhyk*, 'your swords?/grooves?/canals? (4.13).

The Recitation and Performance of the SoS

'A lyric—from the Greek *lura*, lyre—was originally a poem meant to be sung to musical accompaniment' (Falk, p. 71). The very title of the SoS defines it as a composition to be sung and performed; and Jewish tradition, which from Rabbi Aqiba onwards frowned on the chanting of the SoS in public houses (Babylonian Talmud, *Sanhedrin* 101a), is witness to the fact that, at least until it was officially objected to in the second century CE, the SoS was recited and performed on certain recurrent occasions. The question is, of course, what those occasions were. In other words, what was the *Sitz im Leben,* literally, 'place in life') or societal context for the recitation of the SoS?

The obvious setting for individual poems seems to be various occasions and stages of courtship, private as well as public. Those, needless to say, are universally recurrent occasions whose time and place cannot be determined specifically. In regard to the whole composition, it has been suggested that it represents a wedding song of some sort—common (Webster), royal (Goulder), cultic (Meek, Pope), or allegorical (Rabin). It is now assumed that the composition and public recitation of poetry were largely practised by professional women; we shall return to this question in Chapter 10, after discussing the points relevant to female authorship and performance of the SoS.

Further Reading

The love relationships:

> F. Landy, *Paradoxes of Paradise: Identity and Difference in the Song of Songs,* Sheffield: Almond, 1983, pp. 61-133.
> P. Trible, 'Depatriarchalizing in Biblical Interpretation', *JAAR* 41 (1973), pp. 42-48.
> Fox, *Egyptian Love Poetry,* pp. 295-331.
> A. Brenner, *The Israelite Woman: Social Role and Literary Type in Biblical Narrative,* Sheffield: JSOT, 1985, pp. 46-49.

Poetic Forms:

> Falk, *Love Lyrics,* pp. 71-79.

The *wasf*:

> Falk, pp. 80-85.
> Pope, *Song of Songs,* pp. 54-89.
> R.N. Soulen, 'The *wasfs* of the Song of Songs and Hermeneutic', *JBL* 86 (1967), pp. 183-190.

Poetic symbolism and metaphor:

> Landy, see above, and in *The Literary Guide.*
> R. Alter, *The Art of Biblical Poetry,* New York: Basic Books, 1985, Chapter 8, pp. 185-203.

Poetic features and devices:

> D.J.A. Clines (on parallelism, pp. 77-100) and D.N. Freedman (on
>   meter, pp. 11-28) in Follis, *Directions*.
>
> Watson, pp. 87-113.
>
> Alter, Chapter 1 (on parallelism); and see literature cited there.
>
> R.C. Cully, 'Metrical Analysis of Classical Hebrew Poetry', in J.W.
>   Wevers and D.B. Redford (eds.), *Essays on the Ancient
>   Semitic World*, University of Toronto Press, Toronto,
>   1970, pp. 12-28.
>
> Meek, *IB*, pp. 97-98.
>
> R. Kessler (J. Macdonald, ed.), *Some Poetical and Structural
>   Features of the Song of Songs*, Leeds; Leeds University,
>   1957.
>
> S.A. Geller, *Parallelism in Early Biblical Poetry*, Harvard Semitic
>   Monographs 20, Scholars Press, 1979, pp. 5-15 (for units
>   in biblical poetry—couplet, line, strophe, and parallelism;
>   and the bibliography cited).

Setting, recitation and performance:

The topic is closely bound up with two other topics: the literary structure,
and the interpretation of the SoS as a whole. Therefore, additional
bibliographical entries will be listed at the end of the next chapter and
Chapter 8. The question of performance will be discussed again in Chapter
10. Meanwhile, a few recent examples of studies on the settings, or broad
cultural context, reflected in the SoS will suffice.

Domestic context:

> C. Meyers, 'Gender Imagery in the Song of Songs', *HAR* 10 (1986),
>   pp. 219-221.

Common wedding:

> E.C. Webster, 'Pattern in the Song of Songs', *JSOT* 22 (1982),
>   pp. 87-88.

Royal wedding:

> Goulder, *The Song of Fourteen Songs*, pp. 3-4, and pp. 80-87
>   (setting of the SoS in Israelite life).

Liturgical, cultic context:

> Meek, *IB*, pp. 94-96; and see Pope, pp. 145-153.

Modern comprehensive interpretation:

> C. Rabin, 'The Song of Songs and Tamil Poetry', *Studies in
>   Religion* 3 (1973-74), pp. 205-19.

3

UNITY AND SEQUENCE, OR AN ANTHOLOGY? INDIVIDUAL POEMS AND LITERARY STRUCTURE

T HE PROBLEM OF RECOGNIZING the demarcation lines between individual poems is bound up, perhaps paradoxically, with the problem of recognizing the general principles of literary organization that inform the SoS. On the one hand, the boundaries and themes of single poems ought to be identified before the overall structure is defined. On the other hand, once we assume an overall structure of some sort, individual poems are delineated and interpreted according to the hypothesis of structure. The recurrence of poems and catch phrases, either placed symmetrically in the first half of the book (before 5.1, which refers to love's consummation through a drinking/ eating metaphor) and in its second part, or sprinkled throughout the book adds to the problem (see Chapter 2). This phenomenon too may be interpreted in either of two ways—as the random result of collection, or as 'meaningful' (deliberate) repetition. Ultimately, most readers are not satisfied with the thematic unity (variations on erotic love) and, therefore, tend to search for surface unity in the form of a narrative or plot. It must be admitted that some individual poems, once their limits and themes are defined, lend themselves to such plot organization. Others, once again, defy it. Because of these difficulties, there is no consensus among critics on either the number of the poems in the SoS, or on its literary structure. To quote Pope (p. 40): 'The question of literary integrity is bound up with the problem of form and purpose of the book and on all these points there has been and there remains a wide variation of opinion. The conventional division into eight chapters. . . is useful only for text reference'.

Pope (pp. 40-54) supplies a general survey of the problems of defining individual poems and structure under the heading 'Literary Integrity', in which he cites samples for the diversity of views held by scholars. The reader is referred there. The discussions here will be confined to a few points that seem to require further elaboration.

Division into Individual Poems

The number of individual poems distinguished by scholars in the SoS varies greatly. Some examples are: 31 poems (Falk), 29 (Gordis), 20 (Herder), 14 (Goulder), 6 (Exum). This short list demonstrates how difficult it is to assign limits to each poem. As stated above, the difficulties involved stem mainly from two groups of factors: (a) the lack of formal poetic divisions within the Hebrew text; (b) the complex considerations of form, style and content that inform the attempt to delineate any single poem.

Some of these considerations are: the identification of the situational context; the social and geographical background; the speaker(s); the tone and mood (longing, joyous, serious, teasing, and so on); formal features (type of poem); central motifs, metaphors and symbols; specific themes and subject matter; parallels between poems.

Examples

In order to illustrate the problem, let us survey a few passages. 1.15-17 is a dialogue between a male and female lover, as indicated by the use of grammatical gender—male speaker to female listener (v. 15), female speaker to male listener (v. 16). Both speakers refer to each other by 'you are fair' (vv. 15, 16). The imagery is that of the garden/orchard. The theme: love out of doors. But who speaks the last verse (17), which is in the first person plural—the male lover, the female lover, or both in unison? And what is the connection with the next dialogue (2.1-3), whose imagery changes to that of flora and fruit? In this case, one might say that the general theme—enjoyment of love—expressed through admittedly different images is reason enough for stringing the two poems one after the other. What is the connection, however, with the next poem (2.4-7), a monologue in which a maiden speaks about her love-struck condition to the 'Daughters of Jerusalem', and whose background is urban? Perhaps it is the word 'apple' which appears in both poems (vv. 2, 5); but this is a rather shallow sort of linkage. 2.8-13 is, once more, a dialogue of lovers. It celebrates love and spring through an appropriate imagery of flora and fauna; how does it connect with the previous section? And vv. 14-15: how does v. 15 ('Catch the foxes, the little foxes!') relate to v. 14 ('Oh my dove')? Is the latter passage one dialogue poem (Gordis) or two separate poetic monologues (Falk)? The next poem (2.16-17) is a female monologue which, like 2.8-13, refers to the male lover twice by *dwdy*, 'my love'—but in v. 16 he is referred to in the third person, whereas in v. 17 he is addressed directly. The next section (3.1-4) is a search dream, in which a female lover looks for her beloved. It is well-defined as a separate unit by its refrains, repetitions and plot. Its link with the previous passage, however, is superficial, since in the final verse there the male lover is urged to depart. So far, then, the links between poems are effected by catch phrases or similarity of subject matter or imagery, but not of plot.

The foregoing are illustrations of association by verbal and thematic links through a large block of text. A few words about the repetitions and their structural significance are appropriate at this point.

In consecutive passages, verbal repetition is considered an associative device when other criteria (change of speaker, shift of format, change of background, and so on) indicate the beginning of a new poetic unit. In the above-mentioned passages, as in others, repetition of catch phrases facilitates the formation of a chain. Thus the allusion to 'pomegranates' and 'vines' in 7.13 leads to similar ones at the beginning of ch. 8, which is defined by a different situational context as a separate poem; the 'mountain' and 'hill' at the end of a *wasf* (4.6) lead to another poem mentioning the hills of Lebanon and Hermon (4.8), which in turn is linked to the next two poems (4.9-11 and 4.12–5.1) by the epithets 'my sister, my bride'. Such repetitions, nonetheless, do not seem to have any overt narrative significance; they constitute an aid to association and memory, but no more.

Assigning value (or lack of value) to 'symmetrical' repetitions across the SoS is a different matter. On the basis of these Exum divides the book into six poems, disregarding the division by scenes and speakers, and postulating a unity of authorship and design for the whole of the SoS. Landy arrives at similar conclusions through another route, and so does Trible (see Chapter 10). Both Landy and

Exum thus uphold the traditional view in regard to the literary
integrity of the book through modern modes of analysis: the results
of their critical investigation resemble those arrived at by proponents
of holistic interpretations of the SoS, although their methods differ
(Chapter 8).

Some strings of poems indeed exhibit a tighter arrangement, for
instance, 5.2–6.3. Another search dream (see 3.1-4) at first fails (5.2-
7), after which comes a short conversation between the searching
woman and the Daughters of Jerusalem (5.8-9). These offer to
participate in the search and ask for the male lover's description. The
answer is given in the form of a *wasf* (5.10-16). The female chorus
now reaffirms its commitment to help, but needs to know where the
male lover has gone (6.1). He has departed for his 'garden', answers
the girl, and a reunion of the lovers is finally achieved (6.2-3). Thus
at least three poems of three distinct types—a dream poem, a
dialogue with the female chorus, and the embedded *wasf*—are
combined to produce a narrative sequence (or, according to Falk,
pp. 77-78, a single complex poem).

The Overall Literary Structure

Is the SoS, then, a unified sequence of love lyrics, with an ongoing
linear plot? Or an anthology whose components (the single poems)
are linked by some means of association?

Let us return to Exum's work for a moment. She discerns six
poems in the SoS, which are—according to her—arranged in a
chiastic (symmetrical) order. On the basis of this she judges that
unity of authorship and an intentional design exclude the opinion
that the SoS is an anthology or collection. The implication for
exegesis is plain: a unified literary structure indicates a unified
composition, requiring a comprehensive interpretation. In so doing,
Exum gives up the convenient criteria of division into scenes by
changes of speakers, context and so on in favour of an ultimate
solution. As Falk points out, however, no narrative 'plot' has been
suggested, nor has Exum actually advanced an exegetical theory for
the SoS as a whole. Furthermore, the arrangement into chiastic
symmetrical units might be the work of a skilful compiler who strung
together single poems by exploiting associative chains. Therefore
Exum's study, based on stylistic grounds, remains unconvincing, as
do other attempts at assigning a unified design to the whole
composition.

Similar criticism obtains in regard to other interpretations of the SoS as a linear plot sequence. Every attempt at defining a unity of plot—to be distinguished from unity of theme or parity of motif—is uncertain, since it is incomplete and can be ascribed to a compiler as well as to an original author. This is the case with Goulder's proposed plot of a love story between an Arabian princess and King Solomon, whose culmination is the princess's becoming Solomon's queen. Viewed in this way, the supposed plot takes many a dramatic turn and is less than convincing. Landy's treatment, an attempt to demonstrate a structural unity though on a deeper psychological as well as a rhetorical level, confines the love lyrics to a single couple— hence, it accounts for the variety of mood and content only in part. Earlier studies are conditioned by the need to find a focus for the SoS, some kind of unified theme(s) and coherence. Hence, they tend to overlook difficulties in favour of a preconceived theory.

Conclusions

Pope says (p. 54): 'The present writer agrees with Haupt in appreciation of the charming confusion in the Canticles and has not been convinced by any of the efforts to demonstrate or restore order or logical sequence and progression'. With Falk, one must agree that content is no less a key to structure than form. Division into individual poems and the problem of structure are interwoven. Associative principles account for the limits of poems and for their being strung together equally well. Repetitions of catch phrases and even poems may be meaningful thematically, but not necessarily on a 'plot' level. An overall plot for the whole book seems forced. Nevertheless, *some* extended units (made up of smaller ones) seem to exhibit a scheme of events. A surface structural coherence/'integrity' is compatible, or at least reconcilable, with the principles of association described, although it does not automatically indicate an intentional design. In short, it is better to view the SoS as an anthology of love lyrics, which has been compiled according to theme and motif rather than of plot.

The view adopted here, that the SoS is an anthology of love poetry, is known in biblical scholarship as the 'verbal' interpretation. It has been defined partly through reference to modern comprehensive treatments. Other traditional and modern theories of comprehensive interpretation—allegorical, dramatic and cultic—will be introduced in Chapter 8.

Further Reading

Pope, pp. 40-54.

Falk, pp. 62-70.

Landy, pp. 33-58, 137-79.

J.C. Exum, 'A Literary and Structural Analysis of the Song of
      Songs', *ZAW* 85 (1973), pp. 47-79.

W.H. Shea, 'The Chiastic Structure of the Song of Songs', *ZAW* 92
      (1980), pp. 378-96.

Gordis, Chapter 7.

F. Landsberger, 'Poetic Units within the Song of Songs', *JBL* 73
      (1954), pp. 203-16.

4

EXTRABIBLICAL
PARALLELS

L OVE POETRY, like love itself, is a cultural universal. So are its themes: mutuality, passion, wonder, intimacy, adoration, physical appearance of the object of love and its effect on the lover, yearning, suffering, joy, sadness, and so on. Hence, on the thematic level, even on the motif level, the SoS can be compared with any love poetry in the world, old and new. Even the imagery of love lyrics cuts, in many cases, through geographical, chronological and cultural barriers. A substantial degree of resemblance between the SoS and love poetry of other sources is therefore obvious.

The question is, nevertheless, how will a comparison between the SoS and parallel love poetry specifically benefit the reader of the SoS? In other words, (1) what are the parallels that advance our understanding of the uniqueness of the biblical love poems in some manner, and (2) can we establish a connection, some contiguity between so-called parallels and the SoS?

To quote Gordis (p. 30),

> The universality of love as an emotion and an experience, which is responsible for the absence of any considerable degree of specific Hebrew colouration in the book, should make us wary about postulating direct borrowings from other peoples in these songs. Mere resemblances of theme are not sufficient. What is methodologically required is a special sequence of theme or some other unusual feature, not explicable in terms of Hebrew background.

Thus only when direct literary borrowing, one-directional or mutual influence, or extraordinary similarities of structure, theme and content can be pointed out is the comparison worth undertaking.

Correspondences with the following literatures are usually cited for the SoS: ancient Ugaritic, Sumerian, Akkadian, and Egyptian poetry, either secular or cultic; ancient Arabian, modern Arabian and

Druze poetry; ancient Greek; Indian and Tamil. The geographical
and chronological distances covered are thus great but, quite often,
immaterial as such. The diversity of provenance has relatively little
significance since the poetic conventions of subject matter and style
are dictated, to a large extent, by the universal experience of erotic
love and its attendant emotions. The comparisons demonstrate, for
instance, that many images and expressions are shared by the SoS
and by love lyrics of diverse cultures. The depiction of the two lovers
as a shepherd and shepherdess (a poetic convention which lasted in
Western poetry into the Renaissance period and beyond it); the
epithets 'brother' and 'sister'; eating/drinking and vegetation imagery
for sexual passion and its fulfilment; love experienced as a fatal
illness; descriptions of a lover's physical beauty (Paul)—these and
others are common motifs which are relevant but, because of their
wide-spread distribution, hardly particular enough for a useful
comparison with the SoS.

It seems, then, that the customary enlisting of broad parallels
across borders and times, although helpful for placing the SoS within
ancient and more recent cultural contexts, is too general to be deeply
relevant. What matters is the more specific analogies, those that
illuminate poetic facets of the SoS. At any rate, suggested and
verified parallels classified according to their sources have received
wide coverage in scholarly literature (see the Reading list at the end
of this chapter). Therefore, we shall here confine ourselves to a brief
presentation of just two relevant categories of example: (a) love
imagery and its (extralinguistic) sources; (b) genres, contexts, style.

a. Love imagery and its sources

The imagery of the SoS is rich and varied, drawing on many aspects
of human experience of the world and human culture (see Chapter
5). Natural phenomena, zoology, botany, minerals, agriculture, art,
commerce, and architecture are exploited as raw material and
converted into a tapestry of images and symbols designed to convey
love by appealing to and flooding the senses. This 'flooding' of the
listener/reader with sensuous and sensual imagery is a basic trait the
SoS shares with other love lyrics. Most images are recurrent within a
continuous Eastern-Mediterranean-European tradition (see above).
Some of them, however, show a possible literary link between the
poetry of the Hebrews as exemplified by the SoS, and of neighbouring

societies. The resemblance in these cases goes beyond the universality of subject and theme, and implies similar articulation of poetic images.

Let us consider, for example, the passage in which a young woman is likened to a fortified wall (8.9-10). The primary association the image evokes is that of defensibility and chastity, an association which moves from military building to social attitude. A literary parallel, if not actually a source—as distinct from 'source' in terms of literal meaning—for the image can be found in Akkadian incantation texts, which use the same *ḫwmah//dlt*, 'wall//door' imagery (Gordis, after Tur-Sinai and Ebeling). Thus the Akkadian texts, though of a different genre, supply a parallel that assists in the exegesis of a SoS passage.

The depiction of lovers within nature and in harmony with it is indeed universal, but is especially prevalent in Egyptian love poetry. This correspondence to the SoS, together with some other shared epithets, features and attitudes, make Egyptian love poetry valuable for the understanding of many aspects of the SoS (Gerleman, Fox).

Another example is the physical imagery of the male love-object in the *waṣf* of 5.10-16. Verses 11, 14-15 refer to the loved person's head, torso, hands, and legs in terms of precious stones and metals (in contradistinction to the first part of the poem, where fauna and flora govern the imagery). The language of the passage suggests an underlying image of a statue made of several materials (like the statue in Daniel 2.32ff.). The general impression of the description is rather precious, albeit cool and statue-like rather than alive. Such a description of a loved one might seem strange. Therefore, it helps to know that an artistic and poetic convention is reflected here. Mesopotamian literary sources indicate a cultic connection of sacred marriage for similar descriptions within *waṣf*-style hymns, and Ugaritic statues are evidence for the custom of making a god's statue from diverse materials (Pope after Herrmann and Hallo).

b. Genres, contexts, style

The recognition of the *waṣf* genre in the SoS was gained through the knowledge of the same genre in Arabic poetry, as the term itself indicates. This contributed towards the comprehension of other love lyrics of the ancient world and facilitated fresh comparisons which, in their turn, had consequences for further study of the genre in the SoS (4.1-7; 5.10-16; 6.3-7; 7.1-7).

Wetzstein pointed out that the lovers' stylised praise for each other's appearance is similar to the *waṣfs* of wedding couples in Syria. From Budde onwards, the analogies between the praise for the lovers in the SoS and the *waṣf* genre have been given consideration. As various translations by Dalman, Jastrow, and Stephan (see the quotations in Pope) demonstrate, the Syrian and Palestinian *waṣfs* illuminate several features of their Hebrew counterparts. The order of references to parts of the body, the types of imagery employed, the setting (a wedding?), the attitudes, the sexual passion that underlies the aesthetic description—these and other aspects are an important contribution to the interpretation of the parallel SoS passages.

Gordis acknowledges the definition of *waṣf* for 5.10-16, the only poem of the genre which has a male lover for an object. He then cites an ancient Babylonian incantation for recovery, on the basis of which he cautiously assumes that the biblical poem uses the form of the incantation for healing the lover's sexual potency. Hence, two parallels from two cultures are utilized to clarify the passage in question (Arabic poetry and Akkadian charm formulas). Pope goes one step further: he links healing incantations with magical statues made of metals; the making of such a statue in the Sumerian Gilgamesh epic; and the image of Baal, Canaanite god of fertility. To sum up, in this particular case three literary forms (*waṣf*, incantation, epic), three literary cultures (Mesopotamian, Palestinian ancient and recent), another biblical passage (Daniel), and archaeology (Mesopotamia, Ugarit) are cited as parallels for illumination of an SoS passage.

The *waṣf* of 7.1-7 is different from its predecessors in the SoS, among other things by the reverse order assumed for the woman's charms—from toe to head. This unusual order is explained by some commentators as dictated by the situation: when a woman dances, her feet are called to attention first. It is worth noting that the Hindu hymn for the love goddess Parvati (fifth century CE; the translation is quoted by Pope) follows the same reverse scheme and that in it, as in the biblical poem, the female object of love is described in motion. Hence, two *waṣf*-type subgenres can be isolated through the juxtaposition of the SoS and other literatures. The first is inspired by a statue and consequently refers to the beloved in repose, from head to toe, whereas the second refers to her in motion, and from toe to head.

An interesting problem is that of the situational context of love poetry, whose imagery and form closely or loosely resemble that of poems within the SoS, and of the implications of the context for the original setting of the SoS. Sumerian, Babylonian and Ugaritic poems devoted to the gods raise the question of an original cultic-liturgical base for the SoS, whereas the Syro-Palestinian context of wedding songs supports a branch of the theory of dramatic interpretation (Chapter 8).

A cursory glance at the copious parallel material reproduced in Pope's commentary shows that in most instances the love poems cited are in the conventional form of a monologue or soliloquy. Therefore, the dialogues of Egyptian love poetry are (once more, see pp. 29-30 above) of especial value for the SoS, since in both literatures the dialogue format is more frequent. Another important feature of the Egyptian parallels is that at least some of the poems seem to have been collected early, perhaps even primarily designed as components of an anthology.

Ugaritic poetry and the Hebrew Bible share affinities of literary character, style, and language. Some stylistic patterns of SoS poetry are therefore common to both literatures. The correspondences— mainly matters of couplet and stanza structure, repetitive structures, parallelism, recurrent word pairs, common expressions and images— establish a continuous tradition of poetry and its conventional patterns in Ancient Canaan (Cassuto, Avishur).

Rabin's study of Tamil love poetry and its possible links with the SoS and its world is of interest on several counts. First, it contributes towards the understanding of how, where and when the many far-eastern commodities mentioned in the SoS could have been familiar to Hebrew poets. Second, it has implications for the setting of the composition, its literary structure, and date. And third, it offers a comprehensive theory of interpretation.

Finally, there remains the temptation to compare the SoS with modern (post-Renaissance) love poetry. The leap in time and place is justified by the universality of reciprocal sexual love and its literary expressions; but, in my view, it is illuminating for the SoS only when a well-defined feature is looked for. For instance, the erotic imagery practised by the English so-called Metaphysical poets may shed some light on the history and legitimacy of the allegorical (religious) interpretations for the SoS as well as on the process of transition from secular to religious poetry, a transition which retains the

original imagery while displacing it from its original milieu of
metaphorical eroticism. Similary, some Shakespearean love sonnets
seem especially relevant: Sonnet cxxvii—'In the old age black was
not counted fair'—for the dark versus fair ideal of beauty (SoS 1.5-6);
and Sonnet cxxx—'My mistress' eyes are nothing like the sun'—for
the (admittedly disorderly, by biblical standards) *wasf* form and
jocular mood comparable to SoS 7.1-7.

Similar and other instances from Western cultural traditions, as
well as African and American, of love lyrics may undoubtedly be
cited, and to great cultural and personal advantage. The relevance of
any parallels for the understanding of the SoS lies in their relative
specificity—be it a particular image, an attitude, a form of speech,
genre, a point of style—rather than in their universality.

Further Reading

Paul has a comprehensive bibligraphical list for the parallels on p. 655. The
list is arranged according to the place of origin of the parallels.

> Pope, pp. 54-89, quotes extensively from collections of Arabic
> (Jastrow, Stephan), Akkadian, Sumerian, Ugaritic and
> Indian poetry. On pp. 535-50 he comments on 5.10-16
> and deals with the image of the statue.
> Gordis, pp. 30-35 (on the limited advantage of drawing parallels
> and the *wasf* of SoS 5.10-16).
> Brief parallels can be found in *ANET*, p. 496 ('Love Song to a
> King', Sumerian), pp. 467-69 (Egyptian love songs, cf.
> Fox).

For Budde's view of the SoS see:

> K. Budde, *Das Hohelied*, in the series *Die Heilige Schrift des AT*,
> Tübingen, 1923.

Out of the wealth of scholarly literature cited by Pope and Paul, the
following are worth a special mention. The so-called parallels they offer are
supplied with English translation, together with discussions of their value for
SoS study.

For cuneiform texts:

> S.N. Kramer, *The Sacred Marriage Rite: Aspects of Faith, Myth,
> and Ritual in Ancient Sumer*, London, 1969, pp. 85-106.
> W.G. Lambert, 'The Problem of the Love Lyrics', in H. Goedicke
> and J.J.M. Roberts, *Unity and Diversity: Essays in the*

History, Literature and Religion of the Ancient Near East,
  Baltimore and London, 1975, pp. 98-135.
J.M. Sasson, 'A Further Cuneiform Parallel to the Song of Songs?',
  ZAW 85 (1973), pp. 359-60.

For a brief but clear survey of the 'Stylistic Affinity between the Song of Songs and Ugaritic Literature' see (in Hebrew) Y. Avishur in Fox and Klein (eds.), *Shir Hashirim*, pp. 22-23. For affinities between biblical and Ugaritic poetry in general see M.D. Cassuto, *Biblical Literature and Canaanite Literature* (in Hebrew), vols. I and II, Jerusalem: Magnes, 1972, 1979.

For Egyptian love poems:

Fox and the literature cited there.

For Tamil love (*Akam*) poetry:

Rabin, *Studies in Religion* 3 (1973-74), pp. 205-19; and the response by P.C. Craigie, 'Biblical and Tamil Poetry: Some Further Reflections', *Studies in Religion* 8 (1979), pp. 169-75.

The latest and most comprehensive study on the SoS and Tamil Poetry is:

A. Mariaselvam, *The Song of Songs and Ancient Tamil Love Poems*, Analecta Biblica 118, Pontifical Biblical Institute Press, Rome, 1988.

The book has translations of Tamil love poetry and presents the latter's affinities with the SoS. Rabin's and Craigie's positions are discussed by Mariaselvam on pp. 279-86.

5

DAILY LIFE:
SETTINGS, CONTEXTS,
THE ENVIRONMENT

THE SOS HAS SOCIO-HISTORICAL as well as aesthetic and religious significance. Love is obviously a matter of psychological state, but also of reciprocal (social) attitudes. The SoS deals with this primary social subject in a fashion that appears to be relatively non-biased and open-minded. Therefore, it is a valuable source of information in regard to physical realia and societal/social norms. Its worth for the naturalistically and anthropologically inclined reader is enhanced by the fact that the information supplied is not tendentious. Similar data gleaned from the historiographical books of the Bible are often suspect, since they are transmitted within passages that might have been motivated by ideological, social, religious, or political preconceptions and designed to influence the reader's worldview. In the SoS, such information is incidental to the main concerns of the poems. We have already mentioned the absence of specific religious and national contexts in it. Hence, the book may serve as a more credible witness to the knowledge and perceptions of the people who created the poems which it comprises. It may be presumed that the wealth of information contained in the SoS reflects the actualities underlying the various poetic units and the book as a whole. Despite the many clues, however, placing the knowledge gleaned within plausible chronological frameworks is far from simple. Therefore, the value of information about realia for the dating of the book (see Chapter 6) or sections thereof is rather limited.

Nature and the seasonal changes; geography; wild and cultured vegetation; wild fauna and domestic animals; agriculture; urban and rural life; economics and commerce, local and international; social institutions; clothing and jewellery; building and fortifications; military equipment; attitudes to love and sex; aesthetic values—this is just a partial list of the natural and cultural aspects of life that are referred to in passing. The information afforded, from the nomenclature to the descriptions (whether direct or within metaphors), is rich and varied. In the following sections we shall look at some of it.

Nature and seasonal changes

Outside the SoS, there are only two terms in the Hebrew Bible that name seasons: *qys*, 'summer, summer fruit' and *hrp*, 'autumn, rainy period of the year'. The SoS contains two more terms: one specific—*stw*, 'winter' (from the Aramaic; BDB, p. 711 and Pope); and one more general—*zmyr*, 'spring' ('first pruning'? 'singing'? See the debate in Gordis, pp. 6-7 and Pope, pp. 395-96). The description of spring and the phenomena which signify it in nature (2.10-13) follows the universal convention of associating spring and renewal with young love. The celebration of a potential new human beginning is reflected in and refracted from nature, especially through its botanical and zoological aspects. Another description of spring, signified by flowering and blossoming, is the short poem of 6.11 (see Falk's translation).

Geography

The geographical terms in the SoS—cities, localities, mountains, hills, plains, valleys—are amongst the few typically Hebrew features of the book. The places mentioned serve as either background or metaphors for the love poems, thus supplying national colour for the otherwise universal themes (Gordis, p. 25).

Most of the toponyms mentioned are from Northern Israel. They range from the Lebanon and Hermon mountains (4.7-8) in the far Israelite north, to Heshbon (7.5) and Gilead (4.1, 6.5) in the east (Transjordan), through the central Israelite territory (Carmel, 7.6; Sharon, 2.1; Tirzah, 6.4), to the Judaean south of Jerusalem/Zion (3.5, 10, 11; 5.8; 6.4) and Ein Gedi (1.14) on the Dead Sea. Damascus (7.5), Arabia (1.5 and, possibly, the *ndyb* of the obscure 6.12b and 7.2—see Gordis, p. 93; Goulder, pp. 51-52) and Egypt (1.9) are within the metaphorical horizons of the poems. Arable land, natural forest, grazing areas and desert; water sources; rural and urban habitation—all serve as backdrop for human love.

Most of the toponyms mentioned can be identified although others, like *hry btr* (2.17), *bt rbbym* (7.5) and *b'l hmwn* (8.11), do present a problem of identification.

Flora and fauna

The names of various plants and animals which appear in the SoS, unless they appear in other biblical passages too (vines, date palms, lions), may present us with problems of botanical and zoological identification. Nature features in the SoS copiously 'in foregrounds and backgrounds, as real, metaphorical, and symbolic' (Falk, p. 97). Thus, the text does not always permit the classification of a plant or an animal; and the use of these terms as imagery may equally be conventionalized or idiosyncratic. What is the point of comparing the male lover's lips to *šwšnym* (5.13), for instance—the colour, the smell, the appearance of his lips? The term is indeed supported by an Egyptian cognate; its meaning in Hebrew, however, does not necessarily correspond to that of the source language. 'Lotus' (as in Egyptian), 'lily', 'narcissus' are some of the identifications offered. Recently, the identification as 'iris' has been advanced. At any rate, a white flower is invoked here. And what about the *nmr* (4.8)—is it our 'panther', or 'leopard' (see Pope for the verse)?

To sum up. The difficulties arise from our lack of better knowledge concerning the natural habitat of ancient Palestine; the rare terms used; and the confusion caused by the reallocation, in modern Hebrew, of some of the biblical terms to animals and plants that certainly did not exist in the biblical world (for instance, *tpwḥ* in modern Hebrew signifies 'apple', but in the SoS another fruit tree).

Wild and domestic animals

Predatory mammals mentioned in the SoS are lions (4.8), leopards (or panthers, 4.8), and foxes (jackals? 2.15). Gazelles, hinds, and deer do extensive service as similes, metaphors, and symbols (2.7, 9, 17; 3.5; 4.5; 7.4; 8.14; and see below). Of the birds the dove (2.14, 4.1, 5.2, 12; 6.9), turtle dove (2.12), and raven (5.11) are cited.

The domestic animals named are sheep (1.8; 4.2; 6.6), goats (4.1; 6.5), and a mare (1.9). It is difficult to know whether the 'milk' mentioned in 4.11 and 5.1, 12 is sheep's or goat's milk.

Vegetation: Trees, shrubs, bushes, flowers

The image/symbol of the garden/orchard is central to the SoS. A specific place—a vineyard, a natural forest, a (metaphorical) perfume garden—is cited in some instances, while in others the denotation of 'garden' is more general (1.6, 14-17; 2.1-3, 15; 4.12-5.1; 5.13; 6.1-3,

11; 7.8-9, 12-14; 8.5, 11-12, 13). The SoS, then, bursts with vegetation.

Pride of place in the list of flora is given to fruit-bearing trees and plants. These include: apricots/peaches? (*tpwḥ* 2.3, 5; 7.9, 8.5); vineyards, vines and parts thereof (1.6, 15; 2.13, 6.11; 7.8-9, 13; 8.11-12); date palms (7.8-9); pomegranates (4.3, 13; 6.7, 11; 7.13; 8.2); walnut (6.11); and fig tree (2.13). Wheat (7.3) should be added to the list. Aromatic plants comprise a special, well-developed category. They usually carry the same names as those of the products derived from them—hence, whether wild or cultivated, they will be listed under the 'products' heading.

Wild vegetation includes thorns (2.2), *dwd'ym*—'mandrakes'? (7.14), and river rushes (6.11); cedars (1.17, 5.15, 8.9) and firs (1.17). However, the more important representatives of this category are wild flowers which carry a significant symbolical sense but, as stated above, are not easy to identify: *ḥbṣlt* (crocus? lily? rose?—2.1); *sẃśn* and *šwśnh* (lily? narcissus? lotus? iris?—2.1-2; 4.5; 5.13; 6.2-3; 7.3).

Vegetable-derived products

The honey referred to in 4.11, like elsewhere in the Hebrew Bible when just 'honey' is mentioned, is probably date honey. 'Oil' (in the singular and the plural) is perfumed oil (1.3; 4.10) rather than the food product, as indicated by the contexts in which it appears. Wine, from grapes (1.4; 4.10; 5.1; 7.3, 10; 8.2) and also pomegranates (8.2) features largely.

Many aromatic plants used for the preparation of perfumes (and spices—1.12-14; 3.6; 4.6; 4.12-5.1; 5.5, 13; 6.2; 8.14), together with perfumed oils, were known to the poets of the SoS. Few other passages in the OT exhibit comparable knowledge of aromatics and their Hebraized foreign names, most of them imported from Arabia and South East Asia (Brenner). *nrd*, 'nard'; *kpr*, 'henna', *krkm*, 'saffron'; *qnh*, 'cane'; cinnamon; myrrh; aloes; frankincense—all are quoted by name.

Perfumes are a luxury item in any civilization. Such knowledge thus indicates an economically sophisticated, probably urban, cultural context. The original geographical habitat of many aromatics together with their foreign names, which can be related to Dravidian or Sanskrit, is used by Rabin as an argument for the possible existence of trade relations between Israel and Southern India via Arabia in King Solomon's time, hence also for a Solomonic dating of the SoS itself (Chapter 6).

The flora/fauna symbolism

Our survey shows that some images of flora and fauna are recurrent and appear in clusters, whereas others are occasional only. The perfume- and spice-garden which occupies the centre of the SoS (4.12–5.1), encircled as it is by references to eating and drinking (4.11; 5.1a), is an obvious symbol for the consummation of sexual love. The deer or fawn is a symbol for the male lover, while the female lover's breasts are repeatedly likened to 'twin fawns'. The female is a flower or flowers, a garden (of *šwšnym*, 'irises' or perfumes), into which the male lover enters and roams. The vineyard and orchard symbolize a searching for and reciprocal gratification of mutual sexuality and sensual delight.

The recurrent symbols—especially the garden/orchard, and the animal=male/flower=female dichotomy—are interpreted by Landy and others as indications of the literary and structural unity of the SoS (Chapter 3). It must be remembered nevertheless that the recurrence of poetic images may be conditioned by the subject matter or motivated by poetic convention (Chapter 4 above). The universality of the theme, together with principles of associative compilation, explains the repetitions of central symbols as efficiently as a theory of literary unity.

Economics

Proceeding from the nature imagery, one can start to reconstruct an economic profile of the societies reflected in the SoS. These societies were rural but also urban. The economy was mainly based on agriculture—cereals, fruit trees, animal husbandry. Trade was both local and international: wood from the Lebanon; perfumes and spices from the Far East and Arabia; metals (gold and silver: 1.9; 3.10; 5.11, 14-15) and gems (5.14); marble (5.15); and expensive cloth (crimson—4.3; 7.6; purple—3.10; 7.6).

There are terms for jewellery and the raw materials from which it is made (gold and silver, 1.11), terms which are not always easy to equate with archaeological finds. Rich neck and breast jewellery is implied by the image of the female whose neck seems like military fortifications (4.4). Additional terms for female jewellery and clothing are to be found in Isaiah 3 and Ezekiel 16. Terms denoting building and fortification—materials, walls, towers, pools (4.4, probably 6.4; 8.9-10)—and military equipment bear witness to the arts, crafts, skills, and professions practised in the societies whose images live behind and inside the SoS.

Social institutions, mores, and behaviour

Even if we do not subscribe to the traditional view that King Solomon wrote the SoS, or disagree with the 'royal wedding' theory concomitant with it, there is no doubt that Solomon and his court left an impressive mark on Israelite consciousness throughout biblical times. References to Solomon and his royal establishment, including his celebrated harem (2 Kgs 11), apart from the title, are: 1.4; 3.7-11 (for another royal wedding see Psalm 45, whose date is debatable); 6.8-9; and 8.11-12. A working if naive knowledge of royal behaviour is evident although, of course, this does not automatically imply that poems which include such references were indeed composed in monarchic times. Rather, the royal court is depicted as envisaged by the authors and, Solomon's name notwithstanding, is not period-specific.

Urban life, especially in Jerusalem, features in several poems. The streets are made safe at night by patrolling watchmen, who incidentally guard the morality of the inhabitants, especially the women (3.3-4; 5.7). The 'daughters of Jerusalem' are probably girls of high breeding and status, whose life is leisurely enough to afford indulging in love affairs. There are wine houses, to which young people may go (2.4). The urban ideal of beauty seems to be the 'peaches and cream' one (so also Lam. 4.7), in contradistinction to the rural reality of dark, sunburnt beauty (1.5-6; cf. Lam. 4.8). Knowledge of rural life, of course, is borne out by the poetic convention of describing lovers within a basically sympathetic nature, as a couple of shepherds, and by the choice of rural images for conveying a lover's physical appearance and its impact on the speaker(s) (see the *waṣfs*).

A curious feature of the SoS is the way female lovers refer to their family and home: invariably, these are referred to as 'my mother's house' (3.4; 8.2). Even contexts of a royal wedding or harem are linked with a mother's approval (3.11; 6.8-9). Brothers are a part of the family: they play the traditional role of keeping a sister's chastity intact (8.8-9), and have authority within the family unit (1.6). The epithets 'brother' and 'sister', applied to lovers, are obviously an offshoot from filial relations. And yet, a father figure is totally absent from all the scenes.

Whether this state of affairs indicates that the societies reflected in the SoS were informed by matrilineal or fratrilineal principles is far from certain. After all, the attitudes to love and sex—over and part from the acknowledgement of lovers' need to enjoy their love to the point of consummation—bear the hallmarks of patriarchal society. The tension between the two viewpoints, the private and the social, is never resolved. Nonetheless, it must be admitted that the punishment meted to the girl who breaks the sexual code is not too severe (ch. 5); and the women, by and large, enjoy the freedom to look for their lovers and co-operation in the quest from female friends and mothers (Chapter 10).

Attitudes to human aesthetics

As expected within the context of love poetry, physical beauty and sex appeal are much noted and dwelt upon. Female beauty is especially important, although male appearance too comes in for quite a share of praise, both conventionalized (in the *waṣfs*), symbolical (fawn/deer), and free (1.16; 5.10). The emphasis on a female lover's beauty and sex appeal is in stark opposition to another OT voice, which states what is required of a married woman, namely, that loveliness and beauty are of no consequence in a worthy wife (Prov. 31.30).

It has been noted above that references to female as well as male beauty are often formulaic—done through recurrent, conventional similes and metaphors; and yet, we cannot point to a *single* ideal of human beauty. We get the impression that the black/fair contrast (1.5-6) is sociologically determined, since it probably reflects the difference between a rural and urban ideal of beauty (Lam. 4.7-8). In the case of the male body described in the *waṣf* of 5.10-16, part of it has the cool beauty of a sculpture, part the vivid appeal of flesh and blood. If we compare the female *waṣfs* of 4.1-7 and 7.1-7, we find two ideals of female beauty, each expressed by a different tone—the first a partial portrait of an admirable but immobile figure (another sculpture?); the second a full and humorous depiction of a somewhat blemished dancing beauty, in which variations in the usage of conventionalized items are introduced.

Further Reading

On flora and fauna:

> M. Zohary, *Plants of the Bible*, Cambridge: Cambridge University Press, 1982.
> Falk, pp. 97-99.
> And in Hebrew: Y. Feliks, *Shir Hashirim—Teva 'Alila Va'alegoria* (The Song of Songs—Nature, Plot, Allegory), Jerusalem, 1974.

On aromatics and perfumes:

> Rabin, 'Tamil Poetry'.
> A. Brenner, 'Aromatics and Perfumes in the Song of Songs', *JSOT* 25 (1983), pp. 75-81.

On architectural imagery:

Meyers, pp. 212-15.

On gender-specific imagery, and imagery in general:

> Landy, pp. 73-92, 137-78.
> Meyers, pp. 215-21.
> Falk, pp. 99-106.

6

THE LANGUAGE
AND DATING
OF THE BOOK

THE LANGUAGE OF THE SOS is a combination of early, late, and 'neutral' linguistic features. It has affinities with Mishnaic Hebrew and with Ugaritic and Aramaic but otherwise there are only a few foreign words or grammatical structures. Yet, numerous linguistic phenomena constitute a departure from the accepted norms and, within the space of 117 verses, fifty words are words which are found nowhere else (*hapax legomena*). How, then, should the language of the SoS be classified in terms of the various stages of what we call 'biblical Hebrew'? In the absence of other convincing criteria for determining a date of composition/compilation for the book and its constituents, a descriptive and chronological classification of its language is of great importance.

Poetic language, and especially its vocabulary, often seems archaic or archaistic when compared with prose that deals with the same subject matter. There are many instances of SoS forms which can be attributed to early classical (pre-exilic) biblical Hebrew, forms which in time became obsolete in favour of later ones. Ugaritic influence also points to a possibly early nature of some passages. At the same time, many linguistic phenomena—of vocabulary as well as phonology, morphology, and syntax—must be understood as deriving from later Aramaic and Mishnaic Hebrew. In view of the numerous passages which manifest an intimate knowledge of the Northern Israelite territory and are at the same time full of linguistic peculiarities, the influence of the little known northern Israelite 'dialect' must be taken into consideration too—and that 'dialect' perforce dates before the fall of the Northern Kingdom at the end of the eighth century BCE.

Naturally late linguistic phenomena should be given much greater weight if their distribution and frequency within a given text are

more than isolated cases (Hurvitz, Polzin). There is no reason why
later texts should not contain earlier modes of speech and style. A
massive presence of late features would be incomprehensible except
as an indication of a late dating for the whole composition.

Another consideration is the difference between the language of
single poems (whose boundaries are not always easy to delineate),
and that of the composition as a whole. Again, a later composition
(and a collection compiled from individual pieces is as much a
composition as if the individual pieces were indeed written by one
person only) might include earlier pieces, while the opposite is less
than probable.

Ugaritic influence

Albright, Cassuto, Avishur, and others have shown how the language
of the SoS abounds with correspondences to Ugaritic poetry.
Phenomena like extended poetic parallelism (1.15; 4.8), fixed word
pairs and metaphors (1.2, 4), prepositions, particles—to name but a
few categories of instances—are shared by both literatures (Chapter
4 above). If Ugaritic poetry is viewed as a representative corpus of
North-West Semitic poetry, the affinities of the SoS with it are not
surprising. At any event, Ugaritic obviously antedates biblical
poetry, which raises the question of its influence on the latter. It
must be said that parallels to Ugaritic poetry can be found in all
strata of biblical literature; however, their density within a given text
(as in the SoS) might be construed as an argument in favour of an
early date (even as early as the Solomonic era, tenth century BCE) for
that text (Segal, Tur-Sinai, Gerleman, Feliks, Goitein, Rabin).

Foreign Words: Persian, Indo-Iranian, Egyptian

prds (4.13), 'garden, orchard' and *'apprywn* (3.9), 'litter, palanquin',
are apparently of Persian provenance, although *'apprywn* was
formerly thought to be of Greek origin (Meek). Their appearance in
the SoS is of limited value only for the dating of the book. It probably
means a minimal Persian influence: a comparison with biblical books
of the Persian period (notably the Esther Scroll, Ezra and Nehemiah)
demonstrates how massive such an influence can be. Its virtual
absence from the SoS signifies a lack of real chronological proximity
between the Hebrew of the book and the Persian language. Even the

many Indo-Iranian terms for aromatics and perfumes which feature in the SoS in an Hebraized form (like *krkm*, 'saffron'; *qnnmwn*, 'cinnamon') cannot be cited as evidence for a dating in the Persian period. Such terms belong to the semantic class of 'culture words', terms that transcend borders and become assimilated loan words together with the products denoted by them. Therefore, they are not period-specific: knowledge of both words and products is attested in royal tribute lists of various empires from the beginning of the first millennium BCE onwards.

The word *šwšn*, 'iris? lotus? lily?', is derived from the Egyptian for 'lotus flower'. We remember that the SoS exhibits interesting parallels of content and style with Egyptian love poetry (Chapter 4). But, once more, the linguistic as well as other parallels are not period-specific: knowledge of Egyptian culture obtained throughout the biblical world and most of its eras.

Elements of Aramaic, and Mishnaic Hebrew

The SoS abounds with Aramaic, late biblical, and Mishnaic Hebrew phenomena. These include points of vocabulary, morphology, and syntax. Thus *ktl* (2.9), 'wall' is the later equivalent of the classical (pre-exilic) *qyr* of the same meaning, and comes into later (post-exilic and post-biblical) Hebrew from the Aramaic; and the root *nṭr* (1.6), 'guard', reflects the Aramaic pronunciation of the classical Hebrew *nṣr*. In morphology, the relative pronoun *še* (with its compounds) is the only relative pronoun to feature in the SoS, apart from the superscription (1.1) which has the earlier relative *'šr*. The first person pronoun *'ny*, which is the exclusive first person pronoun in later biblical and post-biblical language, is used throughout rather than the earlier *'nky*. And in matters of syntax—the usage of infinitives, double genitives (1.2, 3.7, 8.12), and the absence of the early object marker *'t* are characteristic instances. Extensive lists of Aramaic and Mishnaic Hebrew indications in the SoS are recorded by Driver, Paul and Bendavid.

Discussion and conclusions

The late (mainly Aramaic and post-biblical) correspondences of words, forms and grammatical constructions in the SoS cannot be ignored, or merely attributed to late revisions of the material. The

Ugaritic parallels indeed point to a Northern provenance of at least some poems, since a 'Canaanite' influence was probably greater in the north. It is also plausible that some of the so called Aramaic or Aramaic-influenced features are relatively early, the result of the closer geographical proximity and cultural exposure of the Northern Israelites to Aramaic-speaking people, rather than proof for a later influence brought about by the emergence of Aramaic as the common language of the Persian Empire in the West from the sixth century BCE onwards (Pope). Nonetheless, the number and nature of Aramaic-inspired phenomena cannot be written off as manifestations of the Northern Israelite language only.

If we accept that the SoS is a collection of love lyrics, then seemingly early linguistic material found within the collection poses no problem. Such material may indeed be of an early date, in which case it has probably undergone a long process of oral and perhaps written transmission; or else, it may be the result of poetic tendencies to archaize. The evaluation of the relative date of each linguistic item is sometimes difficult. Nevertheless, the accumulation of decidedly late phenomena can neither be ignored nor attributed solely to the process of compilation.

The date of compilation (or, at the very least, final editing) of the SoS in its present form should, then, be defined as quite late—well within the Second Commonwealth (post-exilic) era. Most scholars settle for the fourth to third (Ginsberg) centuries BCE. Since there is hardly a trace of Persian influence in the book, nor a single Greek word, it seems more plausible to assign its language and, therefore, its composition and compilation to the fifth century (together with Albright, Gordis and others).

As mentioned above, some individual poems bear the linguistic and/or historical stamp of an earlier date. The poem of 3.9-11, whose topic is a royal wedding reminiscent of that in Psalm 45, may be one of those; but unfortunately there is no agreement about the date of that Psalm, beyond assigning it to the early pre-exilic period (tenth to ninth centuries BCE). The list of perfumes in 4.13-14 is understood by Rabin as a specific indication of commerce with India, which is reported by the Bible as having existed in King Solomon's time (1 Kgs 10 = 2 Chron. 9). The attribution of 6.4, where the capital cities of Northern Israel (Tirzah) and Judah (Jerusalem) appear in parallelism, to the ninth or eighth century BCE fits the information about Omri, who made Tirzah his capital before building Samaria

(1 Kgs 16), for there is only a small chance that the grandeur of Tirzah would have been remembered long after the fall of Samaria. We notice that in most of these instances linguistic data, even when taken into account, are secondary to other considerations.

To summarize, the linguistic data confirm a relatively late date (fifth to third centuries BCE) for the SoS as a composition. The recognition of poem boundaries and reflected realia assists in the sometimes almost impossible task of assigning dates to individual poems. The suggested date of composition/compilation has, of course, direct implications for the next topic—the question of authorship, or: who 'wrote' the SoS?

Further Reading

Pope, pp. 22-34.
Gordis, pp. 23-24.
Meek, *IB*, pp. 96-97.
Driver, *Introduction*, pp. 448-50.
Segal, 'The Song of Songs', *VT* 12 (1962), pp. 470-90.
Paul, p. 651.
W.F. Albright, 'Archaic Survivals in the Text of Canticles', in D. Winton Thomas and W.D. McHardy (eds.), *Hebrew and Semitic Studies Presented to G.R. Driver*, 1963, pp. 1-7.

In Hebrew, the following studies are worth nothing:

A. Bendavid, *Leshon Miqra' uLeshon Hakhamim (Biblical Hebrew and Mishnaic Hebrew)*, Tel Aviv: Dvir, 1967, vol. I, pp. 74-80.
N.H. Tur Sinai, *Halashon weHasefer (The Language and the Book)*, Tel Aviv: Bialik, 1950, vol. II, pp. 351-88.

On the definitions of classical (pre-exilic) and late (exilic and post-exilic) biblical Hebrew, and the evidence of language for dating texts:

A. Hurvitz, 'Linguistic Criteria in Dating Problematic Biblical Texts', *Hebrew Abstracts* 14 (1973), pp. 74-79.
R. Polzin, *Late Biblical Hebrew: Towards an Historical Typology of Biblical Hebrew Prose*, Missoula: Scholars Press, 1976.

7

AUTHORSHIP:
WHO 'WROTE' THE SOS?

WE HAVE ALREADY SEEN how the superscription supplied by an editor (1.1), although semantically ambiguous, was traditionally interpreted: the authorship of the SoS was attributed to King Solomon.

Some biblical passages, outside the SoS and inside it, at first seem to support such an attribution. During Solomon's reign, Israel and Judah were one realm. Strong traditions define him as a 'wise' man. He asked God for wisdom to perform his royal functions rather than for wordly goods and, therefore, received both wisdom and the material benefits that it entails for its practitioners according to the mainstream of biblical Wisdom literature (1 Kgs 3.4-15 = 2 Chron. 1.7-13; see Chapter 9 below). His so-called wisdom encompassed not only the ability to dispense law and justice, which is exemplified by the tale of his celebrated judgment in the case of the two prostitutes with one living child (1 Kgs 3.16-28). He was famous also for his building enterprises, including the Temple. A direct consequence of Solomon's divinely inspired wisdom was his economic and govern-mental success, which impressed the Queen of Sheba and enlisted her co-operation in matters of international trade in certain commodities—perfumes, precious metals and gems (1 Kgs 9.1-13 = 2 Chron. 9.1-12). Solomon enjoyed political prestige and had extensive international and commercial influence (1 Kgs 9.14-28 = 2 Chron. 9.13-28). His wisdom, again in keeping with mainstream biblical Wisdom values, included rhetorical and literary skills—in this instance, the ability to talk about, and even with, plants and animals (1 Kgs 5.9-14). Finally, King Solomon was famous for his harem of both local and, mainly, foreign wives. His many sexual liaisons are presented not as political in purpose but, rather, as due to a fatal love of women that had political and religious consequences in the division of his kingdom after his death into a North and South, Israel and Judah (1 Kgs 11.1-13). Thus, according to biblical traditions, many details about Solomon's life make his authorship of the SoS superficially credible. Love of love and women, literary skills, knowledge of nature and its 'languages', architecture and building; international trade, the grand urban life, descriptions of the royal court, frequent references to Jerusalem—all these seem to provide circumstantial evidence for this.

Within the SoS and apart from the superscription, Solomon is mentioned by name in several passages. 3.7-11 places him in three situational contexts: royal security (vv. 8-9), bed (7-9), and wedding (v. 11). In 8.11-12, he has a 'vineyard', whether symbolical or real, in the obscure locality of *b'l hmwn*. Less explicit references to 'the king' (Hebrew *hmmlk*—1.4; 2.12), to a royal harem (6.8-9) and to an Egyptian mare (1.9—see Solomon's marital connection with an Egyptian princess, 1 Kgs 3.1; 11.1; and his chariotry and horses, 1 Kgs 10.26) seem to strengthen the 'Solomonic' aura of the SoS. In addition, some commentators interpret the epithet 'the Shulammite', applied to the dancing woman of the *wasf* in 7.1-7, as a feminine form of *šlmh*, Solomon.

In Chapter 6 we have established that it is impossible, on linguistic grounds, to assign the date of the SoS to the tenth century BCE. In its *present form*—undoubtedly the end-product of a complex transmission process of which we know little, but the only text we have to go by— it is so replete with late semantic and grammatical phenomena that a post-exilic date for the composition as a whole is obvious, although not necessarily for several specific poems. Let us now see how the references to King Solomon and his assumed authorship of and involvement in the SoS can be explained.

Whenever Solomon is referred to within the SoS, this is done in the third person singular. It stands to reason that an author is not likely to do this but, rather, that he would normally use the autobiographical 'I'. When the word *hmmlk*, 'king' appears, it might signify a soubriquet, a nickname for a bridegroom, as in some Arab wedding poetry. The same explanation would account for references to women as princesses, or as harem women; one does not have to subscribe to the dramatic-wedding theory of the SoS (Chapter 8 below) in order to use this argument. Other Israelite and Judahite kings enjoyed international influence, trade and other connections apart from Solomon: in more than a few instances, while biblical tradition omitted such information for religious reasons, extra-biblical sources supply it. (Ahab is a case in point, cf. 1 Kgs 16–22 with the Assyrian chronicles; and some scholars attribute Psalm 45, which celebrates a royal wedding in terms similar to those of the SoS, to his time). The luxury items and geographical horizons (Chapter 5 above) also fit a post-exilic chronology, when relatively open frontiers within the Persian Empire were the norm. Other kings too possessed horses and chariotry and indulged in building projects (notably Ahab again, 1 Kgs 22). The derivation of 'the Shulammite' (7.1) from *šlmh* is dubious. The references to Solomon in particular and to the pre-exilic monarchy in general are a-historical, for they do not impart knowledge of specific data. In short, it is plausible that a well educated, well informed author/compiler of the Persian period could easily pick up diverse popular, even 'Solomonic', love poems and weave them into the *present form* of the SoS text, an anthology of love lyrics.

The collection as it now stands contains poems of various styles, varied backgrounds, and different dates. The author/compiler (or additional persons) probably undertook some editing and editorial decisions too—which explains the overall symmetrical structure and a certain cohesion, however we choose to interpret that cohesion (Chapters 3 above and 8 below). Thus, a general framework was apparently supplied by the person responsible for the collection. Unfortunately, the identity of that person (or those persons, for the activity of a group rather than an individual should not be ruled out too casually) cannot be uncovered. Let us just say that his/her/their anonymous activity should be dated to the fifth to third centuries BCE and, as supported by the text, that this was carried out within the local Jewish community and geographical boundaries of the Persian era in Palestine.

There is a growing tendency nowadays to attribute the SoS, or at least substantial portions thereof, to a *female* author/editor or authors/editors. Female authorship would clarify some of the outstanding features of the composition, such as the predominance of female figures, the bold directness of female voices (although this features in Egyptian love poetry too, Chapter 4), the prominence of the mother and her 'house', and the lack of a father figure. The question of female authorship for the SoS will be further discussed in Chapter 10 ('Feminist Readings'). Meanwhile, we may conclude by saying that even though the author's/authors' gender (and date) may be defined with a certain measure of accuracy, an exact or even approximate identity is impossible to achieve.

Further Reading

Ginsburg, p. 124.
Gordis, pp. 18-23.
Meek, pp. 96-97.
Goulder, pp. 72-74.

On the literary activities of women and female authorship in the Hebrew Bible:

S.D. Goitein (trans. M. Carasik), 'Women as Creators of Biblical Genres', *Prooftexts* 8 (1988), pp. 1-33.

8

THEORIES OF COMPREHENSIVE INTERPRETATION

THE TRENDS OF INTERPRETATION introduced below share an assumption which is prior to exegesis—that the SoS is a *unified* work in the compositional or, at the very least, editorial sense. These interpretations are based on the hypothesis that the SoS has a *unified*, , not just integrated, structure. This structure is assumed to carry a central theme, a central plot, and a central message. The principles of organization that inform the order of the poems, including the repetitions, are perceived as much more meaningful than merely associative. In other words, the form of the book is interpreted as a frame whose significance is more than the sum of its parts. Hence, the results of comprehensive exegeses—unless they are firmly anchored in the purely linguistic and structural levels of investigation (Exum, 1973)—tend to depart from a primary level of understanding towards some core of a hidden, symbolical or representational, understanding.

In Chapter 3 it was argued that the SoS is best viewed as an anthology of lyrics whose subject matter and theme is sexual love, and whose components (individual poems) are strung together by various and fairly loose principles of organization. This 'verbal' or 'literal' interpretation implies that the text should be taken at face value and interpreted accordingly. It must be pointed out that such an approach does not necessarily exclude additional levels of interpretation: implicit, 'secretive' meanings may be inherent in a text side by side with the more obvious explicit meanings (Kermode). Although we can seldom speak about the presumed authors' intention with any degree of certainty, informed reader's response must be part of our understanding of a literary text. Therefore, the SoS may be simultaneously interpreted, theoretically at least, on more than one level (Rabin). The literal meaning is then not denied but a 'higher', religious significance is sought for the whole composition (Calvin). Methodologically, however, the legitimacy of derived 'meanings' is secondary to that of the primary, literal meaning.

It is necessary to recognize that even the verbal content and meaning of the SoS (erotic love) is culture-bound. This meaning ought not to be considered so 'secretive' that it would generate a consistent comprehensive interpretation of a text. Nevertheless, it is helpful to remember that the SoS is perforce rooted in its Israelite and ancient Near Eastern cultural contexts (Ginsberg; Chapter 4). Against the background of those contexts human love may be referred to in terms of divine love, fertility cults, and religious rituals celebrating the cycle of life and death (Pope). The echoes of such contexts, when understood by the reader as clues for a 'higher' meaning, facilitate attempts at comprehensive interpretations.

Allegorical/Symbolical Interpretations

The allegorical and symbolical interpretations of the SoS originate in antiquity and constitute an attempt at fitting the book into an orthodox religious framework. It seems fair to assume that they were motivated, at least partly, by the unease with which ancient commentators viewed the secular and overtly sensuous character of the poems. Love in the SoS is therefore transformed through interpretation into an exclusive love *story* between two specifically defined partners. Turning attention from the secular relations of mere humans towards the relations between the divine and the human seems to supply a missing link and to justify the book's canonical status (Chapter 1), inasmuch as it continues pagan traditions of divine-human love lyrics (Chapter 4).

Five features are shared by most of the Jewish as well as Christian exegetes who have followed the allegorical methods.

1.   The SoS has two main 'characters', one male figure and one female figure.
2.   A single, continuous plot is assumed for the whole composition.
3.   The love relationship is reciprocal and legitimate, symbolical of a relationship between the divine (male) and a specifically designated community of faith (female).
4.   The interpretation accounts for as many details of the text as possible.

5.   Consequently, departures from the literal meaning (Hebrew
          peshat) are unavoidable, and the resulting interpretation is
          more than a trifle forced.

In the extrabiblical book called *The Apocalypse of Ezra* (4.24, 26
(*The Apocalypse of Ezra*, or *4 Ezra*, is a Jewish book dated to the end
of the first century CE, whose subject is the destruction of Jerusalem
and the Second Temple by the Romans in 69 CE), the community of
Israel is designated 'dove' and *šwšnh* (lily? iris?), symbolical attributes
gleaned from the SoS. That is the first evidence for symbolical
interpretations of the SoS, interpretations which came into vogue
between the fall of the Second Temple and the Bar Kokhba revolt in
132–135 CE. The SoS is understood to be an allegory, mystical and/
or symbolical, for the love story between God ('Solomon'; *dwd*,
'lover'; 'shepherd') and the community of Israel ('sister'; 'bride'; 'the
Shulammite'; *r'yh*, 'companion'). By the time of Rabbi Akiba (50–
132 CE), the allegorical elaboration has supplanted the literal one and
has become the favourite and even the only legitimate interpretation
of the SoS, so much so that R. Akiba considered the book to be one of
the utmost religious importance (Mishna *Yadayim* 3.5; Chapter 1).
Midrashic and Talmudic literature abounds in historical-allegorical
clues for the divine/human love relationship: so in the *Song of Songs
Rabbah*, the Aramaic Targum to the SoS, and the *Taanit* Scroll (4.8).
(The *Taanit* Scroll (Heb. 'Fast') is a tractate of the order Mo'ed in the
Mishna, Tosefta, the Jerusalem and Babylonian Talmud, dealing
mainly with fasts and days on which fasting is expressly forbidden).
    The tradition of comprehensive symbolical-allegorical interpretation
was continued by the Jewish exegetes of the Middle Ages (Rashi and
others), when some commentators (Ibn Ezra, Isaac and Judah
Abrabanel, and others; see Ginsburg) added a philosophical touch to
the allegorical approach. Jewish mysticism, which supplies God with
a female companion called *Shekinah*, 'dwelling (entity)' or 'Matron'
(and finally the Shabbath), treats the union of the two divine
elements in obvious sexual terms. The practice of referring to the
divine couple by erotic language was probably made possible by the
tradition of the allegorical interpretation of the SoS, as well as by
memories of extrabiblical love lyrics (both human and divine) and
the psychological need to complement the Godhead with a female
element (Patai).
    The Church Fathers adopted the allegorical mode of interpretation
during the third century CE. Their specific applications of it vary—

from a dialogue between Synagoga and Ecclesia to a love story of Jesus and the Church, God and the human Soul, and Jesus and the Soul. Other Christian interpretations posit Mary at the centre of the SoS, identifying her as its Shulammite/female lover and also as the Church. Origen, Jerome, and Augustine supported variations of the allegorical trend of interpretation with such dedication that, at least in some orthodox circles, it remained prevalent until fairly modern times. However, since Herder introduced his literal interpretation (1778; see Pope), the allegorical explanation of the SoS has gradually been abandoned.

In a sense, the allegorical description of the divine-human relationship in terms of an erotic liaison harks back to OT prophetic traditions. Passages in Hosea, Jeremiah, Ezekiel, and Second Isaiah depict the relations between God (the male) and his people (the female) through the metaphors of sex and marriage. Nevertheless, the affinities between that prophetic poetic convention and a comprehensive understanding of the SoS as an allegorical love story are superficial only. To begin with, marriage does not seem to be at issue in the SoS (but see below); other differences and similarities between the prophetic traditions and the allegorical mode will be discussed in Chapter 9.

In general, both Jewish and Christian allegories attributed to the SoS suffer from the tendency to over-symbolize and thus depart further and further from the primary, literal level of comprehension and exegesis. The credibility of such interpretations is hampered, at least for most modern readers, by their religious bias. Historically, however, allegorical interpretations are important, since they served as the single or most dominant mode of exegesis for hundreds of years.

Ginsburg and Pope include detailed surveys, arranged in chronological order, of both Jewish and Christian allegorical and symbolical interpretations in the Introductions to their respective commentaries.

Dramatic Interpretations

Some manuscript traditions of the Septuagint, from the fourth and fifth centuries CE, already assign the verses of the SoS to specific speakers. These manuscripts foreshadow the view, advanced by Jacobi and others in the eighteenth century and especially developed by Delitzsch (1875) and Ewald (1826, 1876), that the SoS is a drama.

The dramatic readings, like the allegorical ones, are based on several assumptions which inform the procedure of interpretation.

1. The SoS has literary integrity—it is one composition throughout.

2. It has a unified, linear plot. The plot can be divided into dramatic segments—acts and scenes. The text is viewed as a dramatic script. Thus, the assumed plot movements are explained through reference to conventions which govern dramatic presentations. In other words, since the actual text of the SoS is not written as a dramatic script, a certain amount of reconstruction has to be done and stage instructions have to be supplied in order to reproduce a 'play'.

3. The speakers who voice poetic dialogues, monologues, soliloquies, and choral responses are not merely a poetic convention, but a cast of dramatic personae.

4. The plot unfolds the love story of a single couple. Hence, there are two main characters, male and female (Delitzsch); or a romantic triangle of two males and a female (Jacobi, Ewald, Driver).

In most of the interpretations in this category, the literary persona of the dominant male lover is King Solomon. The female lover is socially inferior—a rural shepherdess, a girl from Shunem (=Sulam, thus a 'Shulammite'), or a foreign princess (Goulder). The drama is presumably the story of these two unlikely lovers, whose culmination is a conventional happy ending. When a romantic triangle is postulated, the third character is a shepherd, to whom the girl returns in spite of the temptation presented by Solomon's love and his rich Jerusalem court. The reader is referred to Driver for short synopses, divided into acts and scenes and with general instructions for stage and settings, of the two-character (Delitzsch) and three-character (Ewald) alternative scripts (Driver, pp. 438-43).

The shortcomings of the dramatic theories of interpretations cannot be ignored. The major critical objections levelled at them are as follows (Rowley, Gordis). The various plots suggested, together with their formal division into dramatic segments, are far from convincing. The stage directions supplied are imaginary. It is clear that a literary unity of the SoS, unless attributed to an editor/compiler, is impossible for linguistic reasons; consequently, a unified drama is ruled out. Moreover, it is questionable whether full scale dramatic presentations were practised by the Hebrews in OT times before well into the Hellenistic period. In short, the dramatic theory, together with its various mutations, is finally no more acceptable than the allegorical methods of interpretation.

Cultic Interpretations

In the twentieth century it has become popular for scholars to regard large portions of the Bible as cult material, adapted and reworked from neighbouring cultures. Accordingly, the SoS is interpreted as a religious-literary reflection on or transformation of a liturgical composition, assimilated into Hebrew literature from an external Near Eastern source.

Suggestions of provenance for the myths involved and their representation vary. Egyptian, Babylonian, Sumerian and Canaanite sources are quoted. All the suggestions share a basic premise: the SoS originates in a story whose plot is the ritual representation of the *hieros gamos* (sacred marriage) of a fertility god and goddess, which is part of the recurrent cycle of the death and rebirth of the fertility god. In other words, cultic interpretations claim to reveal a hidden historical and religious meaning that underlies the text. In that sense they are, to quote Gordis, 'The most modern force of the allegorical theory', one which 'regards our book as the translation of pagan litany' (Gordis, p. 4). In the sense that they include the idea of representation, such interpretations are also offsprings of the dramatic theory.

De Jassy (1914) started the trend by explaining the SoS as an Egyptian liturgical text connected with the Osiris ritual. In his interpretation, the loving couple of the SoS are transfigurations of Osiris=King Solomon and the goddess Isis=the Shulammite.

Meek's interpretation (from the 1920s onwards) is the most popular example of this kind of theory. According to him, the SoS originated in the Babylonian liturgy of the Tammuz-Adonis and Ishtar cult, processed and adapted to the popular Israelite practice of worshipping fertility gods, a practice much denounced by various prophets (Hosea, Jeremiah, Ezekiel; see the next chapter). Here too Solomon and the Shulammite represent the male and female divinities; and the plot recounts the fertility god's cyclic death and rebirth, which symbolizes the cycle of vegetation and fertility in nature and was therefore celebrated in a recurrent annual festival.

Kramer at first objected to the cultic theories of Meek and his followers, because his studies of Sumerian and Akkadian sources did not yield literary evidence of Dumuzi-Tammuz's resurrection. As Yamauchi shows (1965; see Pope, p. 153), Kramer's objections greatly weakened the cultic theory. Later (1969), after new Sumerian texts had been discovered and interpreted, Kramer suggested that at least some of the poems in the SoS should be linked with a Hebrew version of the sacred union myth, a version which originated in the Sumerian Dumuzi-Innana myth and was assimilated into Israelite culture through the mediation of the Babylonian and Canaanite myth and ritual.

Pope, like many other commentators, sees SoS 8.6c-d as the climax of the whole book ('for love is strong as death, ardour/jealousy harsh as the grave'). He does not attempt a detailed comprehensive interpretation, but nevertheless links the book with ancient Near Eastern funerary rites. He cites biblical, rabbinical, Christian, Mesopotamian, and mainly Ugaritic sources to support his theory. In his own words, he suggests that 'certain features of the Song of Songs may be understood in the light of the considerable and growing evidence that funeral feasts in the ancient Near East were love feasts celebrated with wine, women, and song' (Pope, p. 228). And he summarizes, 'The connection of the Canticle with the funeral feast as expressive of the deepest and most constant concern for Life and Love in the ever present face of Death adds a new insight and appreciation of our pagan predecessors' (p. 229). Pope's interpretation is thus a variant of the cultic theory, although it shifts the emphasis from the fertility aspect of the myth to its death and resurrection aspect.

Critical objections to the cultic theories of interpretation are many; some of them will be listed here. Read literally, the SoS contains no clue for the death and resurrection myth of a fertility god. The reconstructions of that same myth in Mesopotamian and Ugaritic literature are far from certain. Human love is the subject matter of the biblical poems, not divine love. On the contrary: there is no overt divine element in them. Could a text celebrating foreign rites and festivals have been accepted into the official scriptures of Judaism? The Jewish liturgical reading of the SoS on Passover is so late (see Chapter 11) that it cannot be adduced as evidence for a liturgical origin of the text. Moreover, the cultic theories posit a male figure at the centre of the composition, thus failing to account for the predominance of the female in it. Finally, the cultic approach is religiously biased. It seems to be conditioned, consciously or otherwise, by an analogy drawn between Jesus and ancient fertility gods, whose hypothetical resurrection myths are interpreted as a foreshadowing of Christ. Detailed critiques of the cultic theory are given by Gordis and Rowley (see Further Reading).

Wedding and Wedding Week Theories

At the end of the nineteenth century Wetzstein published his work on village weddings in contemporary Syria. The wedding lasts a 'royal week'. The bride and bridegroom are treated as king and queen, and *wasfs* (Chapter 3) are sung in their honour. The bride herself performs a dance. No wonder that the SoS *wasf*-like poems (4.1-7; 5.10-16; 6.4-7) and the dance poem (7.1-7) were compared to the Syrian custom (Chapter 4). Budde popularized the view that the SoS is an ordered collection of ancient wedding songs, sung during the wedding feast. In the first half of the twentieth century a considerable number of scholars subscribed to the notion, which presupposes a fixed order of the poems and a central theme and movement of the 'plot'.

Some scholars still subscribe to variants of the theory, which appears to be a secular version of the cultic theory (marriage rites) combined with the dramatic interpretation (division into related poetic sequences). For example, Goulder (1986, p. 71) claims that 'the Song is a single poem, and not a collection of love lyrics: it moves through a sequence of fourteen scenes from the [Arabian] princess's arrival in Jerusalem to her acceptance as Solomon's beloved Queen' (cf. Goulder's table of individual songs and replies by the chorus, also p. 71).

Jewish sources indeed demonstrate that during the Second Temple era the bride was praised and addressed in song; the bridegroom was likened to a king; both parties wore diadems (SoS 3.11); and the bride was carried in a palanquin (3.9). However, no proof for the usage of the SoS as a comprehensive text for wedding ceremonies can be adduced from these sources (Paul, p. 650). Further, an analogy between Arab poetry of the nineteenth century, traditional though this may be, and the SoS seems justified only by the general subject matter. And again, a literal reading of the SoS excludes the theme of marriage as a principal factor in it.

Structural Interpretations

The quest for methodological principles, with the intention of establishing a unity of authorship and poetic design for the SoS, has been undertaken in recent decades mainly through the application of form criticism. Some samples of this scholarly trend will be given below.

Segal (1962), who admits oral transmission for the poems and a complex editorial process, still maintains a basic plan for the book up to 5.2 (Love's consummation). He classifies the rest of the poems as later versions of the poems of the first part, thus accounting for the repetitions and apparent lack of 'plot' in the second part.

Exum (1973), starting from a critique of Angénieux's articles (in the 1960s), postulates a chiastic structure of six poems (1.2–2.6=8.4–14; 2.7–3.5=5.2–6.3; 3.6–5.1=6.4–8.3). She concludes that the structural analysis proves unity of authorship and design, but stops short of an actual exegesis (p. 79). It must be pointed out, however, that the structure does not exclude editorial rather than authorial unity (Falk; Chapter 3).

Landy, following Murphy (1979), Exum and Shea (1980), also proceeds from a structural analysis of the SoS, especially the feature of chiasm. He then treats the book as a unified composition, reading it as a text concerning the relationship between a single pair of lovers, with recurrent symbols and concerns. This assumed continuity enables him to embark on a reading informed by psychological and psychoanalytic theories.

Trible (1973, 1978) views the SoS as a therapeutic answer, admittedly incomplete, to the patriarchal biblical myth of the Garden (Gen. 2.4b–3). She too assumes one couple, one erotic love, in the SoS. Her work will be further discussed in Chapter 10.

Conclusion:
In Favour of a Literal Method of Interpretation

The comprehensive interpretations surveyed in this chapter are primarily motivated by two wishes: to establish a literary cohesion for the book; and to reveal a uniform principle of organization, preferably of a 'higher' significance, that transcends the basic level of erotic love. Although such interpretations may satisfy our aspirations for order, meaning and coherence, they do not withstand criticism well. What remains is to return to a 'simple' verbal or literary interpretation, that is, to view the SoS as an anthology of profane love lyrics loosely—if often meaningfully—strung together. The rest, the attribution of 'intention' or 'design' to the original composition and its components, is a matter of reader's perception rather than of verifiable theories.

Ever since antiquity, a minority of Jewish and Christian exegetes

have admitted the secular nature of the love lyrics preserved in the
SoS. Since the eighteenth century, this trend has gained more and
more ground. This notion does subvert notions of a 'higher' or
'transformed' meaning. Its implications for the question of literary
integrity are clear—it makes it easier to relegate authorial unity to a
secondary position of editorial activity. In spite of this drawback, at
present the verbal interpretation seems the best and least fanciful
solution for the comprehension of the SoS (Ginsberg).

Further Reading

F. Kermode, *The Genesis of Secrecy: On the Interpretation of
        Narrative*, Harvard University Press, 1979, discusses the
        notion of an 'inside' and 'outside' interpretation.

A literary-critical reading of SoS imagery, performed from within the
framework of Christian thought and tracing the path of allegorical
interpretation, can be found in:

N. Frye, *The Great Code: The Bible and Literature*, New York:
        Harcourt Brace Jovanovich, 1982, ch. 6 (especially
        pp. 140, 154-56).

A recent instance of a comprehensive, self-professed 'double meaning'
analysis (allegory and literal interpretation uneasily combined) is:

R.J. Tournay, *Word of God, song of Love: a Commentary on the
        song of Songs* (J.E. Crowley, trans.), New York and
        Mahwah, NJ: Paulist Press, 1988.

Detailed surveys of methods for comprehensive interpretations of the SoS
are given by Pope, pp. 34-37, 89-229; Ginsburg, pp. 20-124. The surveys are
classified and, for the most part, arranged in chronological order.

Rowley, *Song of Songs*, pp. 195-246 and Gordis, pp. 2-14, supply
        valuable criticism of the methods discussed.

Additional material on the cultic theories:

O. Neuschatz de Jassy, *Le Cantique des Cantiques et le Mythe
        d'Osiris-Hetep*, 1914.
R. Patai, *The Hebrew Goddess*, New York: Avon Books, 1978.
S.N. Kramer, *The Sacred Marriage Rite: Aspects of Faith, Myth,
        and Ritual in Ancient Sumer*, Bloomington: Indiana
        University Press, 1969.

T.J. Meek, 'The Song of Songs and the Fertility Cult', in W.H.
Schoff (ed.), *A Symposium on the Song of Songs*, Oriental
Society of Philadelphia, 1924, pp. 48-79.

A succinct summary in favour of the literal interpretation of the SoS is
Ginsberg's Introduction to the Jewish Publication Society of America
translation (see General Reading List), pp. 3-4.

For comprehensive interpretations of the 'verbal' variety which are
informed by stylistic and structural considerations see, apart from Exum
(1973) and Segal (1962): J. Angénieux, 'Structure du Cantique des
Cantiques', *ETL* 41 (1965), pp. 96-142 and 'Le Cantique des Cantiques en
huit chants à refrains alternants', *ETL* 44 (1968), pp. 87-140; R.E. Murphy,
'Form-Critical Studies in the Song of Songs', *Interpretation* 27 (1973),
p. 413-22; 'Towards a Commentary on the Song of Songs', *CBQ* 30 (1977),
pp. 482-96; and 'The Unity of the Song of Songs', *VT* 29 (1979), pp. 436-443;
W.H. Shea, *ZAW* 92 (1980), pp. 378-96; Landy, pp. 33-58.

9

INTERTEXTUAL CONNECTIONS:
THE SOS WITHIN THE
BIBLICAL CONTEXT

SECULARITY, A-HISTORICAL CHARACTER, lack of national bias, and the theme of love are characteristic of the SoS. The accumulative weight of these four features makes the book unique within the literature of the Hebrew Bible. Because of this uniqueness, it is especially important to view the book against the background of other biblical passages and other literary genres.

I have chosen to discuss three points in order to demonstrate that, in spite of its unparalleled character, the SoS has strong affinities with diverse biblical traditions. The first relates to the thematic level—erotic love, intersexual relations, expressions and manifestations of love relationships—in prophetic texts. The second is a matter of genre: it links the poetry of the SoS with biblical Wisdom literature, with which Hebrew poetry is generically associated. Finally, the story of the Primaeval Garden (Gen. 2.4b–3.24) has pronounced affinities with the SoS, among which are the features of a-historicity, non-national approach, and intersexual relationships. Therefore and for other reasons, a juxtaposition of the two texts is indispensable for the comprehension of each one, and of both.

Love Texts in the Prophets:
The Case of Male Love and Female Fickleness

Hosea was the first prophet, as far as we know, to use the bold imagery of heterosexual love for the depiction of the relationship between the Hebrew God and his people (chs. 1–3). The relationship between God and his chosen people is formalised by means of a covenant, and metaphorized in terms of marital love and a marital contract (chs. 1–2). God is the devoted, loving, dutiful 'husband'; Northern Israel is the fickle, adulterous 'wife'; the 'Baal' or 'Baals' (in

the plural!) is/are cited as the 'woman's' illicit 'lover/s'. Because of
the heartless 'woman's' behaviour the contractual relationship does
not work. A process of divorce, punishment, isolation, and re-
education is to be applied to the 'woman'-people (2.7-16; ch. 3) before
the legal and loving relationship can be resumed, this time without
hindrance from the reformed 'adulteress'. This time, everybody will
know that love and fertility come from the true God (2.17-25) and
not from illicit 'lovers'.

The bold description is dialectically inspired by the phenomena
Hosea tries to fight—Canaanite fertility cults and their celebration of
the 'sacred marriage' (*hieros gamos*) rituals. The story of the unhappy
affair is delivered by a male voice and from a male's viewpoint. The
woman-people is described as disloyal and emotionally unstable. The
husband-God is a loyal, mature and steadfast lover. Hosea himself is
commanded to take a 'harlot' for a wife, so that his personal life
serves as a symbol for the allegory of the divine, one-sided male love
(1.2, with a different version in ch. 3; see Wolff's commentary).

Hosea's teachings in chs. 1-3 certainly refer to an unhappy love
story. Even without discussing the admittedly interesting question of
the mutual influence between Hosea's actual life and his prophecies
(see commentaries), it is clear that the 'woman' gets short-changed.
The imagery denotes a bitter, unrequited male love. On the surface,
then, there is no connection between the Hosea texts and the SoS
apart from the basic subject matter (love). There is certainly not
much similarity between the Hosean vision of marital non-bliss and
the reciprocal loving that permeates the SoS. Thematically, the two
texts appear to be diametrically opposed to each other. Nevertheless,
it can be shown that, genetically and stylistically, they are related.
Both seem to have originated in a common tradition of Hebrew love
poetry, of which the SoS is the most extensive remnant. Some
passages of both even appear like two variations, done from two
different viewpoints, of the same text. Since the issue here is that of
gender-specific poetry and the values of patriarchy and its institutions,
we shall return to a comparison of the two texts in the next Chapter
(10, 'Feminist Readings').

Hosea lived in the second half of the eighth century BCE
(according to Ginsberg, chs. 1-3 of the book are even earlier and
should be attributed to an anonymous prophet of the mid-ninth
century BCE). The love hyperbole first used in the book so named
persisted through the ages. It was taken up by Jeremiah (ch. 2) who

later in the seventh century BCE, not long before the destruction of Jerusalem and the First Temple, deals similarly with the same religious context of pagan worship which constitutes a breaking of the covenant between God and his people. He extends the metaphor to include an implicit political fickleness and speaks about two equally promiscuous 'women'—Judah and Israel (ch. 3). Once again God is the loving and long-suffering male, and the people an animalistic and lusty female who has to be threatened with divorce (expulsion from the land).

Ezekiel, of roughly the same period as Jeremiah's but living and prophesying in Babylonia, adds his own touch and stronger language to the love imagery. In ch. 16 paternity, another patriarchal aspect, completes the marital picture first drawn in Hosea. God is Jerusalem's adoptive father first, then her loving husband. She betrays him. Her punishment and re-education will be followed by a new and lasting (marriage) covenant. Once more, pagan worship is referred to in terms of the 'woman's' 'harlotry' and 'fornication'. In ch. 23 two sisters/wives are cited, Samaria and Jerusalem, and their 'adultery' is as political—'Assyria' and 'Babylonia' are the 'lovers'— as it is religious (cf. Jer. 3). Here the language is explicitly sexual, vulgar, and openly sexist. God is a true lover. His 'women' are common harlots, adulteresses whose transgressions are punishable by public shame and death, so that women everywhere will stay faithful to their husbands (23.48).

Further usages of the same hyperbole, albeit in a modified form and much gentler language, are to be found in Second and Third Isaiah (Isaiah 50.1, chs. 54 and 62), later in the sixth century BCE. The people, or Zion/Jerusalem, are again a 'woman'—wife, mother, lover. This time, they claim that the husband-God has forsaken them. This time, he promises to reverse the situation and, after the exile, restore the 'woman' to her original status of loved wife (and mother).

We notice that the tradition of the (metaphorical and contractual) love relationship between God and his people remained alive in prophetic expression for hundreds of years. It can be read as a link between the SoS and pagan fertility myths on the one hand, and as early proof for the development and eventual prominence of the Jewish allegorical interpretation of the SoS on the other. In the allegorization of the SoS the personae are, once again, God the male lover and Israel the female lover. The love relationship, however, is transformed. In the SoS, the woman is loyal, loving, active, and honest. The situation between the lovers is actually reversed, for now the woman does more than her fair share of courting. Read as an item belonging to a series in continuity, the SoS is a fitting therapeutic answer, within the biblical framework, to the harsh patriarchal vision of the hetereosexual kind of love imagined by the prophets. Such a reading does not necessarily imply a chronological ordering of the relevant texts: some poems included in the SoS, or similar compositions, might be earlier than at least several of the prophetic passages mentioned. It merely assumes that the love plot presented in each text illuminates and complements, by way of analogy or opposition, love plots in others; and that the theme, literary provenance, and conventions underlying all 'love' passages, if not their emotive contents, basically belong to the same poetic stock.

Poetry, the SoS, and Wisdom Literature

Wisdom in the Hebrew Bible is, first and foremost, the secular knowledge of practical skills. Intellectual prowess, philosophical inquiry, and religious thought are secondary to the pragmatic goal of the *ḥkmh*, which is to acquire proficiency and dexterity at all levels of personal and social endeavour. Rhetoric, poetry and music—together with other public and social skills—are thus branches of 'wisdom', because they are crafts studied and practised like any other craft; so much so, that the existence of guilds of poets and musicians may be assumed for the Hebrews and their neighbours in OT times (Albright, see Gordis).

Poetry, performed to musical accompaniment or recited, with or without dancing, on joyous as well as sorrowful occasions, was an integral part of Hebrew life. Shorter and longer poems, distributed throughout the biblical books, bear witness to that fact. Some passages explicitly define poetry as 'wisdom' (Solomon's wisdom in 1 Kgs 5.10-12=1 Chron. 15.19; Jer. 9.16-20). There is no reason to exclude the SoS from this broad classification.

Several OT passages attribute poetic and musical activities to women, be these activities spontaneous or professional (Miriam's song, Exod. 15.20-21; the women's praise of the victorious David, 1 Sam. 18.7; 21.12; 29.5; Deborah's song, Judg. 5). Jeremiah states explicitly that 'wise' women serve as professional mourners, who write their texts and also perform them. The SoS, with its prominence of female voices and female viewpoints, may just be—at least in part—another female-authored text. If this possibility is found to be feasible, it will supply additional information with regard to biblical wisdom traditions, since most of the teachings in the extant biblical texts reflect and are directed at a man's world. We shall return to this matter again in Chapter 10 below.

The SoS and the Garden of Eden (Genesis 2.4b-3.24)

Gen. 2.4b-3.24 is, among other things, a story about relationships and a 'garden' in which and out of which these relationships develop. The garden image of both Genesis and the SoS is symbolical of the female body, the true beginning of all human existence (Frye, p. 107). Furthermore, a number of items of theme and imagery are shared by both texts. Hence, a comparison of the Eden narrative with the SoS is inevitable, since relationships and gardens are at the centre of both. Beyond the structural framework, however, the attitudes and messages of the two texts are fundamentally different.

In the Garden, the natural order of things is presented in an unnatural reversed manner: the female is born out of the male (Gen. 2.21-22), and the male attaches himself to her (2.24). Then (3.1-7) the first two human beings acquire the divine knowledge of 'good and evil' and human sexuality through the woman's initiative. The outcome of that act of disobedience matches the offence. It proves painful for female sexuality (childbirth) and female social status (3.16), and for the male it means hardship in his ordained role of breadwinner (3.17-19). The patriarchal order of things, and the nature of gender relations, are thus established even before the couple is expelled from the (non-erotic) garden (3.22-24). The garden story therefore tells of the painful side of sexual love and female fate. In Christianity the theme of the guilt/offence/punishment linked with sexuality is taken even further; the garden story is the story of The Fall, for which the woman is roundly blamed.

By contradistinction the SoS is non-sexist and, by and large, non-patriarchal. No female inferiority of judgement, intellect, or emotional make-up is implied in its poems. On the contrary. The females who inhabit the poems are allowed freedom of speech and action. Love brings pain as well as joy, but this pain does not have far-reaching physical and social consequences (5.7-8, where the woman is beaten for raoming the streets at night, but not sexually molested for her immodesty). The pain of love is shared by both sexes (8.6-7). The couples of the SoS freely inhabit their 'gardens', actually and metaphorically, with no divine or paternal force to expel them. If we wish, then, we may view the movements of the love relationship(s) in the SoS as a return to a psychological (internal) Eden through the redeeming power of love. In that other 'garden', sexuality is openly admitted. In that garden, gender inequality, together with material and social conflicts between the sexes, pale into insignificance.

Landy says about the two juxtaposed texts that they are 'Two versions of paradise. . . The primordial couple in Eden lose their Paradise for the same reasons that the couple in the Song regain it. . . Both texts find their complement in the other. . . '. He then goes on to say 'Their opposition conceals a hidden identity. . . ' (p. 183). This last statement, however, is less than satisfactory for feminist readers, whose contributions to the reading of the SoS will be discussed in the next chapter.

Further Reading

For the prophetic books mentioned see the following commentaries

On Hosea:

> H.L. Ginsberg, 'Hosea', *EJ*, Jerusalem: Keter, 1971, vol. VIII, pp. 1010-24.
>
> H.W. Wolff, *The Book of Hosea* (Hermeneia, translated from *Kommentar zum Buch Hosea*, 1961), Philadelphia and London: Fortress/SCM 1974.

On Jeremiah:

> W. McKane, *Jeremiah 1-25* (ICC), Edinburgh: T. & T. Clark, 1986.
>
> R.P. Carroll, *Jeremiah* (OTL), London: SCM, 1986.

On Ezekiel:

> W. Zimmerli, *Ezekiel 1 & 2* (Hermenia), Philadelphia and London: Fortress/SCM, 1979-1983.

On Second Isaiah:

> R.N. Whybray, *Isaiah 40-66* (New Century Bible Commentary), Grand Rapids and London: Eerdmans/Marshall, Morgan & Scott, 1975, reprinted 1981.

For the SoS and Wisdom Literature see Gordis, pp. 13-16.

For the SoS and the Garden story (Gen. 2.4b-3):

Frye, pp. 107-14.
Landy, pp. 183-265.

10
FEMINIST READINGS OF THE SOS

BROADLY SPEAKING, 'feminism' is a system of values and beliefs, that is, an ideological and political system. It recognizes that in our civilization women are unjustly subordinated to men and advocates a transformation of this social situation. Literary criticism is obviously one of the means for effecting a social change, since it deals with the cultural myths we live by. Therefore, in feminist literary criticism—as in any other branches of feminism—the identification and critique of unequal attitudes towards women are given a large place, together with attempts at re-defining women's roles within literature and the social worlds it reflects.

Because the feminist approach entails a total worldview, the literary criticism informed by it tends to be interdisciplinary. It focuses on women and their affairs but is not limited to those, for its aim is to analyse all facets of human behaviour and its expressions.

Several interconnected issues have been on the agenda of feminist research in theology and biblical studies in recent decades.

1. The application of feminist critical theories to the specific fields of bible and theology.
2. The analysis of patriarchy (the socio-political system of male domination over women and minors), androcentrism (the view advocating the primariness of the male sex), phallocentrism (belief that maleness is the norm and a yardstick for judging human behaviour) and related phenomena within religious texts. Because these have served through the ages as justification and means for women's subjection, their analysis is often aggressive and angry.
3. The exposure of sexual politics in the literary characterization of female individuals and female types.

4.   The reclamation of female heritage which, very often, is masked by the (male) texts. The procedure of re-interpretation aims at recovering information in regard to female institutions, social activities, status, self-image, and literary activities.
5.   The re-evaluation of pagan religions and fertility cults.
6.   A re-examination of women and their place in monotheistic religions.
7.   Attempts to re-write biblical interpretation and religious history in a manner that will accommodate feminist sensibilities and contribute towards the correction of the historical and social balance between the sexes.

Applied to the SoS, feminist readings deal with the following specific features: possible female authorship of the book or parts thereof; the lack of sexism (discriminating persons on grounds of their sex, usually used for the social prejudices against women); equality in the love relationship, and predominance of the female figures; elements of matristic practices (power in the hands of women) and matrilineal practices (tracing male kinship and inheritance through the mother's line) as against institutions of patriarchy; gender analysis of female and male discourse, that is, the defining of the emotional and psychological attributes that society expects of its male and female members; comparisons of the SoS with love lyrics of cognate Near Eastern cultures; and investigations into the intertextual connections between the SoS and other treatments of love-themes in the Hebrew Bible.

The list shows that the concerns of feminist criticism partly overlap those of other schools of criticism, but also that they go beyond the more traditional approaches to ask other questions from other angles.

The following notes are intended to point out a number of directions taken in the past and likely to be taken in future feminist research on the SoS, and to demonstrate that a variety of approaches rather than a single approach are implicit in it.

C.D. Ginsburg and His Interpretation of the SoS

In 1857 C.D. Ginsburg published his Commentary on the SoS and Qoheleth (reprinted 1970). In his Introduction to the SoS he has a section called 'Importance of the Book' (pp. 12-20), which is a heated defence of women's reputation in biblical literature and of the view of the SoS as a liberating text. Many issues taken up decades later by feminist readers of the SoS—the intellectual and moral equality of the sexes, the degradation of women in biblical literature and in the cultures related to it, the restored female image in the SoS, the link with the Genesis creation account (1.1–2.4a) and garden narrative (2.4b–3.24)—are forcefully advanced by Ginsburg. In that sense, as Pope has said, he is a pioneer of the feminist reading of the SoS (Pope, pp. 137-41).

The 'Dream' Sequences

In 3.1-4 and 5.2-7 there are two passages which are, perhaps, dreams (see Gordis, Pope, and other commentaries). The speaker in both passages is a female figure, the theme a nocturnal search for the male lover. The ending is different in each case—the search is successfully completed in 3.4 but fails in 5.7, where the woman is beaten for her transgression by the city guardians.

Pusin (Pope, pp. 133-34) has recognized that the two sequences contain classic (related to the unconscious) dream material, and that the dreams, be their author/s male or female, are female dreams representing female inner psychological reality and fears within the social reality.

Female Authorship and Female Culture in the SoS

Literary creativity precedes literary and cultural consumption. The recognition of authorship is therefore a matter of emotional and social concern for both males and females: it legitimizes a person's identity within his/her culture. No wonder that the uncovering of presumably suppressed, obliterated and forgotten literary activities has been one of the chief concerns of women readers.

The Israeli scholar Goitein published in 1957 his theory about 'Women as Creators of Biblical Genres', especially poetry. He proceeded from observing women's literary activity during the first years of Israeli statehood, when ethnic cultural and literary traditions were brought into the country and orally preserved and transmitted by women, even though those women were more often than not illiterate. He then applied his findings to biblical literature and was able to establish female authorship for certain biblical passages

(Goitein: 1957 in Hebrew; English translation 1988). He defines the SoS as a female composition (Hebrew, pp. 301-307) because of its contents (atmosphere, gender equality, predominance of the female, 'answer' to the Genesis garden story) and for more general conceptual reasons (he sees women as the custodians of love poetry in ancient Israel) and analogical reasons (Egyptian love poetry). His approach is now largely accepted by many scholars (Meyers, 1986).

Other discussions of female authorship in the SoS and elsewhere in the Hebrew Bible can be found in Bekkenkamp and van Dijk (1987), and Brenner (1985). In these and other works, the element of female performance of the poems is as much a feature as that of authorship. It is plausible to assume that the SoS and similar love poems—like other biblical poems whose performance and/or authorship is attributed to women—were actually performed on recurrent occasions. We do not have to subscribe to the dramatic or wedding theories of interpretation in order to surmise that love lyrics are recited at weddings, or poems of courtship sung whenever a gathering of young people takes place. Another possible setting for recitations of love lyrics is an all-women gathering. Recognizing the possibility of poetry recitations within such gatherings may explain a large cluster of SoS features (female prominence, outspoken emotions, bold imagery, female authorship, relative lack of concern for male authority).

Intertextual Connections and the Critique of Patriarchy

The patriarchal bias characteristic of biblical literature in general is absent from the SoS. The female figures in it are, to a large degree, autonomous: they are linked to mothers (3.4; 6.9; 8.1-2) and 'mother's sons' = 'brothers' (1.6; 8.1, 8-9), but not to a 'father' and his authority. A female defies her brothers' authority in word and deed; virginity and the segregation of women are mocked (chs. 1 and 8). She also defies the patriarchal code of female modesty when she roams the streets at night, looking for her lover (3.1-3; 5.7). Female co-operation in the quest for the male lover is indicated by the appeals to and responses of the Daughters of Jerusalem chorus (2.7; 3.5; 5.8-9; 6.1, 9; 8.4). The freedom to love and express love is exploited more by the females than the males.

The paucity of patriarchal attitudes and the different vision of social behaviour in the SoS are at least partly explained by the hypothesis of female authorship. Hence, the book provides a good stepping stone for the critique of biblical patriarchal attitudes, especially by comparing it with biblical texts whose male authorship and viewpoints are pronounced.

Trible collates the SoS with the narrative of the garden (Gen. 2.4b–3.24). By juxtaposing the two texts she strives to show how the Bible can be 'depatriarchalized', thus providing a frame of reference for women today (1973, 1978). A non-feminist summary and critique of Trible's 1973 article is to be found in Pope (1977, pp. 205-10). Landy, who treats the theme of the two 'gardens' at length, also frequently refers to Trible's work.

Another line of investigation is to show the intertextual connections between the SoS and the prophetic passages discussed above (in Chapter 9). For example, van Dijk (1989) exposes the patriarchal and discriminatory views of Hosea 2. By defining the Hosean passage as a male love poem and juxtaposing it with the female love lyrics of the SoS, it is possible to point out the differences between these two gender-determined manifestations of the love poetry genre and the social ideologies that underline them. The male love poetry, represented by Hosea 2, is linked with the religion of Yhwh, whereas the female love poetry is linked with the worship of the (fertility) goddess: cultic interpretations (Chapter 8) thus acquire a new coherence.

Style, Discourse, Genre

It is rather curious that, within the mutuality of the love relationships in the SoS, strong 'masculine' metaphors of war and military construction are applied to the female. Meyers (1986) explores the gender-specific imagery of several SoS passages and proceeds to discuss female culture (or, in her words, sub-culture) within a male-dominated (androcentric) world.

The *wasfs* (Chapter 2) of the SoS are spoken by male (4.1-7; 6.3-7; 7.1-7) and female (5.10-16) voices. These poems supposedly describe the lovers. They raise an issue 'which has ramifications for our understanding of the Song as a whole. . . the topic of male and female roles and representations in the Song, and their conformity to stereotypes' (Falk, p. 85). In a discussion of the *wasf* genre, Falk deals with what she calls 'a double prejudice' (p. 86)—that the poet of the

SoS is male, and that the *waṣf* ascribed to a female voice is composed by a female and is inferior in literary quality. As Falk says, such an approach fails to account for the equal attitudes apparent in the text of the SoS, *waṣfs* included. Falk's concluding remarks on this topic should serve as a warning to all readers of biblical literature, and especially the SoS (pp. 86-87):

> Sexist interpretations of the *waṣf*, and of the Song in general, are a striking example of how the text can be distorted by culturally biased reading. To interpret the Song authentically, we must shed the cultural blinders that make what is foreign seem strange. It may even turn out that this ancient text has something new to teach us about how to redeem sexuality and love in our fallen world.

Further Reading

Articles mentioned in this chapter:

P. Trible, 'Depatriarchalizing in Biblical Interpretation', *JAAR* 41 (1973), pp. 42-48.

P. Trible, *God and the Rhetoric of Sexuality*, Philadelphia: Fortress, 1978, Ch. 5, pp. 144-65.

J. Bekkenkamp and F. van Dijk, 'The Canon of the Old Testament and Women's Cultural Tradition', in M. Meijer and J. Schaap (eds.), *Historiography of Women's Cultural Traditions*, Foris, Dordecht, Holland and Providence, 1987, pp. 91-108.

F. van Dijk-Hemmes, 'The Imagination of Power and the Power of Imagination: An Intertextual Analysis of Two Biblical Love Songs', *JSOT* 44 (1989), pp. 75-88.

For samples of basic feminist research on issues mentioned in this chapter, but not necessarily or specifically on the SoS:

P. Bird, 'Images of Women in the Old Testament'; in R.R. Ruether (ed.), *Religion and Sexism*, New York: Simon and Schuster, 1974, pp. 41-88.

J.C. Exum and J.W.H. Bos (eds.), 'Reasoning with the Foxes: Female Wit in a World of Male Power', *Semeia* 42 (1988).

R.M. Gross (ed.), *Beyond Androcentrism: New Essays on Women and Religion*, Missoula: Scholars Press, 1977.

Two useful collections of essays on various aspects of feminist biblical scholarship are:

P. Trible (ed.), 'The Effects of Women's Studies on Biblical Studies', *JSOT* 22 (1982), pp. 1-71.

A. Yarbro Collins (ed.), *Feminist Perspectives on Biblical Scholarship*, Chico: Scholars Press, 1985.

11

THE SOS IN
JEWISH AND
CHRISTIAN LITURGY

In Jewish Liturgy

THE JEWISH SAGES frowned upon the secular recitation of the SoS, to the point that even its study was not encouraged. The prohibitions were undoubtedly caused by the overtly erotic tenor of the poems. Meanwhile, the allegorical interpretation gained ground and became the official teaching (Chapters 1 and 8).

The sacralization of the SoS facilitated its entrance into the liturgical service. The process must have been a gradual one. The book was associated with the season of spring so prevalent in it and consequently at some point it became customary to read it during the Passover Festival. It is generally assumed that the custom is pre-Talmudic and that it originated in Palestine, although the date of its institutionalization remains unknown.

The first evidence for the reading of the SoS at Passover comes from Tractate *Soferim* ('Scribes'), one of the so-called 'minor' tractates attached to the Talmud and dated to the middle of the eighth century CE. It says there that 'In the case of the Song of Songs, it is read on the last [two] nights of the Passover Festival, half of it on the first night and the other half on the second night' (*Soferim* 14.18). A private reading is implied by the text here. Later, it seems that the custom changed. According to the Vitry *Maḥzor* ('Cycle'; a composition which gives the rulings and texts for the liturgy of the whole year; from the beginning of the twelfth century), the SoS had by then been established as part of the Passover synagogue service. It was read on the intermediate Sabbath of Passover, before the Torah Scroll was taken out of its ark. If the festival started on a Saturday, the SoS was read on that day in Palestine, on the last day of the festival in the Diaspora (p. 304).

In certain communities nowadays the SoS is read after the (private) ceremony of Passover night, and on the Saturdays between Passover and Pentecost. Kabbalistic influence was instrumental in instituting another custom—that of the reading of the SoS by some communities in the synagogue on Friday nights before the evening service.

In Christian Liturgy

Christianity adopted from Judaism the allegorical mode of interpreting the SoS (Chapter 8), substituting Jesus and the Church for God and his people (the Christological approach). Another interpretation was to view Mary as the real and mystical bride of God (the Mariological approach). Another further identifies the Christian Soul with Mary/ the Bride. These trends of interpretation were instituted very early by the Church Fathers.

Accordingly, portions of the SoS served not only as texts for sermons but also featured in the liturgy of Marian festivals. The text was that of the Latin Version (the Vulgate). From the fifteenth and sixteenth centuries CE, musical scores were composed for the Marian celebrations.

Statues of Mary from medieval Southern Europe sometimes have a black head. These venerated figures, much prayed to, may constitute a link between the cult of Mary and the worship of the black goddesses in antiquity—from India to Greece and Rome— through the 'black' woman of the SoS (1.5-6), with whom Mary is identified (Pope).

Further Reading

On Jewish liturgy:
The quotation from Tractate *Soferim* is from:

I.W. Slotki, 'Masseketh Soferim'; in: A. Cohen (ed.), *The Minor Tractates of the Talmud*, London: Soncino, 1971, vol. I, p. 282.

See also:

R. Posner, U. Kaplan, S. Cohen (eds.), *Jewish Liturgy: Prayer and Synagogue Service through the Ages*, Jerusalem: Keter, 1975, p. 146.

On Christian liturgy:

> Pope, pp. 183-92, with sample quotations from the Church Fathers
> and others. He also cites extensively from:
>
> P.P. Parente, 'The Canticle of Canticles in Mystical Theology',
> *CBQ* 6 (1944), pp. 142-58.
>
> M. Warner, *Alone of All Her Sex: The Myth and the Cult of the
> Virgin Mary*, London: Picador, 1985 (= 1976), esp. ch. 8,
> pp. 121-33 and the notes on pp. 376f. (on Mary as the SoS
> 'bride' and the Mariological allegorical interpretation).

12

THE SOS IN
MUSIC AND
THE VISUAL ARTS

WE HAVE SEEN that the SoS has been interpreted for centuries as, first and foremost, an allegorical document of symbolical and mystical significance. On the other hand, the literal meaning of the book has always been admitted by a minority of commentators and began to gain wide acceptance from the end of the eighteenth century. No wonder then that in music as well as the visual arts, in the Jewish as well as the Christian spheres, treatments of SoS themes can be grouped under two headings which reflect the division into religious and secular interpretations.

The SoS in Music

The masoretic accents attached to the written text of the SoS imply a certain way of singing. This liturgical 'singing' is probably different from the original tunes of the SoS poems, referred to in the Mishna (*Yadayim* 3.5), and varies from one Jewish community to another. Secular renditions of poems are mentioned too; and in modern Israel, many of the SoS lyrics were given new tunes and a new lease on life as 'folk' and popular songs and dances. Some musical scores by prominent Israeli composers also go beyond the liturgical function, although these can be based on specific liturgical traditions.

In the fifteenth and sixteenth centuries, music for SoS texts was composed for liturgical performances (Marian festivities, see Chapter 11). This practice continued into the seventeenth century (Monteverdi), and later the text was also set to music for weddings (J.C. Bach). With the rise of the secular and dramatic interpretation of the SoS in the last two centuries (Chapter 8) cantatas, oratorios and pieces for choir and instruments were composed.

In the Visual Arts

A sample list of SoS themes in art, from medieval times onwards, is given in the *EJ*, vol. XV, p. 151. Illuminations for the book in Jewish manuscripts, such as the one on the initial panel of the book in the Tripartite *Maḥzor* (colour plate in *EJ*, vol. XI, between pp. 684 and 685), should be added to the list.

Two works seem to illustrate the two main approaches to SoS interpretation, the religious and the secular/erotic. One is a woodcut by Holbein. In it, King Solomon stands in a frozen attitude in the foreground and recites the text, which the title defines as allegorical/symbolical of Jesus and the Church. On the other hand, a series of paintings by Chagall (1923, at the Louvre) discloses a world not devoid of Jewish and Christian symbols but replete with sexuality: strong colours, naked lovers, animals, gardens, plants. Interestingly, in each painting there is at least one tree that is more prominent than the rest. Thus we are led back from the Garden of the SoS to the original Garden of Genesis and to the signification of the Tree of Knowledge, as in a number of modern interpretations of the SoS.

Further Reading

A. Herzog, *EJ*, vol. XIV, p. 1058 (on Jewish musical renditions of the SoS).

B. Bayer, *EJ*, vol. XV, pp. 151-52 (music).

INDEXES

INDEX OF ANCIENT SOURCES

OLD TESTAMENT

INDEX OF AUTHORS